Successful Strategies for

Reading in the Content Areas

Secondary

Shell Educational Publishing

Published by:
Shell Eduactional Publishing

Publisher:
Rachelle Cracchiolo, M.S. Ed.

Curriculum Product Manager:
Karen J. Goldfluss, M.S. Ed.

Editor-in-Chief:
Sharon Coan, M.S. Ed.

Designers:
Lee Aucoin
Phil Garcia

Authors:
Sarah Kartchner Clark, M.A.
Christine Dugan
Teresa Moretine, M.A. Ed.
Jennifer Overend Prior, M. Ed.
Jan Ray, Ed. D.
Mary Rosenburg, M.A.
Andrea Trischitta, M.A./M.A.T.

Editorial Staff:
Sara Connolly
Gisela Lee, M.A.
Elizabeth Morris, Ph.D.

Production:
Phil Garcia
Alfred Lau

Shell Educational Publishing
5301 Oceanus Drive
Huntington Beach, CA 92649-1030
www.tcmpub.com
ISBN-0-7439-0179-7

Reprinted, 2005
Made in U.S.A.

Table of Contents

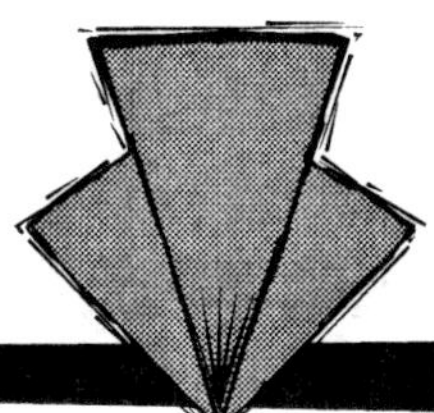

Introduction

Reading comprehension is a complex process involving interactions between the reader and the text, using multiple skills. This process begins before reading, when the reader activates background knowledge. It occurs during reading, when the reader tests that prior knowledge with new information, and it continues even after reading, to enhance comprehension through various post-reading activities.

Students need a variety of strategies to be successful readers. They need to understand the way words are printed on the page, the purpose of printed material, and the relationship between printed and spoken language. They also should be familiar with different writing patterns and styles. Personal experience or knowledge about the topic is helpful.

There are features of the text that can affect comprehension. Sometimes readers find complicated sentences difficult to understand; they need to think about the context of the text to aid in discovering the meaning. There are various ways that text is arranged within a reading selection, and students should be aware of how that information is arranged. An example would be chronologically ordered paragraphs or cause-and-effect paragraphs.

Students can be made aware of these various features of the text through systematic instruction and repeated exposure to a wide variety of reading materials. When a student understands the type and parts of the text they are reading, comprehension is enhanced.

Successful Strategies for Reading in the Content Areas contains a variety of reading strategies that will help increase comprehension. Some strategies include purpose questions, predicting, previewing, anticipation guides, webbing, writing before reading, etc. The book is divided into the following 12 sections:

- Main Idea and Supporting Details
- Summarizing and Paraphrasing
- Developing Vocabulary
- Prior Knowledge and Making Connections
- Author's Point of View
- Structural Patterns
- Using Text Organizers
- Using Parts of the Book
- Making Inferences
- Setting the Purpose
- Questioning
- Visualizing

Each of these 12 sections contains an introduction, teaching strategies, and templates for students. It is important to read the introduction of each section before using the strategies to understand how best to teach these important nonfiction skills. These strategies in this book can activate prior knowledge and give students a purpose for reading. The activities will motivate your students to want to read and understand the text.

The accompanying CD-ROM contains the graphic organizers in this notebook in *Microsoft Word* and *Inspiration* format. You can customize the organizers for your personal classroom needs. See pages 278–280 for an index of these files.

Main Idea and Supporting Details

Main Idea and Supporting Details

Introduction

At the secondary school level, students must be able to identify the main idea in texts across the curriculum. Identifying the main idea provides the cognitive foundation for questioning, visualizing, connecting to prior knowledge, and many other sophisticated reading strategies. Many students will quickly be able to identify the main idea by previewing the text. Other students will need to read carefully, examine supporting details, and make deductions about the main idea. Still other students will struggle with identifying the main idea and need explicit instruction and modeling in order to master this skill. One of the first things teachers must do in their classrooms each year is to diagnose students' abilities in identifying the main idea. Once teachers determine students' needs, they will need to use strategies and instructional approaches that meet the diverse needs of all students. Lessons and activities should reinforce the skills that secondary school students are presumed to have mastered. These skills include identifying the main idea, retelling, finding evidence to support the main idea, and restating facts and details.

Finding the Main Idea

The main idea is the point that the author wishes to make about a topic. It is the central thought or message that readers need to understand. Students also should understand that often the main idea is *explicit*: the author states the central idea within the text. However, sometimes the main idea is *implicit*; that is, the main idea is not stated anywhere within the text and readers must infer the message from the supporting details. The following paragraphs are examples of both explicit and implicit main ideas:

The main idea is first sentence followed by details:

> *Clara Barton, known as America's first nurse, was a brave and devoted humanitarian.* While caring for others, she was shot at, got frostbitten fingers, had severe laryngitis twice, burned her hands, and almost lost her eyesight. Yet she continued to care for the sick and injured until she died at the age of 91.

The main idea is in the middle of the paragraph with details on both sides:

> The coral have created a reef where more than 200 kinds of birds and about 1,500 types of fish live. *In fact, Australia's Great Barrier Reef provides a home for many interesting animals.* These include sea turtles, giant clams, crabs, and crown-of-thorns starfish.

The main idea is the last sentence summarizing the details that came before:

> Each year Antarctica spends six months in darkness from mid-March to mid-September. The continent is covered year-round by ice that causes sunlight to reflect off its surface. It never really warms up. In fact, the coldest temperature ever recorded was in Antarctica. *Antarctica has one of the harshest environments in the world.*

Main Idea and Supporting Details

Finding the Main Idea *(cont.)*

The main idea is not stated in the paragraph and must be inferred from the supporting details:

> The biggest sea horse ever found was over a foot (45 cm) long. Large sea horses live along the coasts of New Zealand, Australia, and California. Smaller sea horses live off the coast of Florida, in the Caribbean Sea, and in the Gulf of Mexico. The smallest adult sea horse ever found was only one-half inch (1.3 cm) long.

In this example the implied main idea is that sea horses' sizes vary based on where they live.

Retelling Key Text Information

The ability to retell is important because it enables students to encapsulate key information as it relates to the main idea and to learn content. Students need to internalize the following questions in order to demonstrate their mastery of retelling:

> What is the key concept or main idea in the text?
>
> What are the important supporting details?
>
> What is the extraneous information?
>
> How can I link the important information together?
>
> How can I relate the information in my own words?

Finding Evidence to Support the Main Idea

In order to make sense of texts across the curriculum, students must also be accountable for finding evidence that supports the main idea. The following are some tips for helping students find key textual evidence when reading:

1. Reread the text, skimming and scanning for important information.
2. Reread the headings and subheadings to determine supporting evidence.
3. Look at the text features and read the captions.
4. Reread the introduction and conclusion for generalizations and conceptual information. Compare and contrast supporting paragraphs.
5. Work with a partner to discuss and find evidence from the text.
6. Read multiple texts on the same topic and compare supporting details in order to discover what is most important.

Main Idea and Supporting Details

Restating Facts and Details

Students must learn to restate facts and supporting details in order to remember important information. Having them categorize facts as they read helps them make inferences about clusters of related words. When necessary, the teacher can give struggling readers the categories before they read and have them sort details or facts into those categories as they read. More capable students can list the facts, categorize, and then reread to see if they missed any information. As students gain independence with this skill, the teacher can have them read short portions of text and identify a category of information and the facts and details that further develop or explain the category. The goal is to help students become readers who automatically sort and organize information in their minds as they read in order to restate the information in a coherent manner. Achieving this goal requires intense strategy instruction and modeling of the strategy by the teacher so that students understand what is expected of them.

Using Graphic Sources

Students at the secondary level will need continuous skill building in using graphic sources. Text that is highly visual and graphic is very motivating. However, it is important that students are able to discern the main idea and supporting details even when previewing, reading, and analyzing graphic texts. Often they will become distracted by highly graphic texts; focus on the illustrations, photographs, and charts; and fail to come away with an understanding of the main idea of the text. Previewing text can solve this problem. Also, use think alouds to model how to identify and retain important information and ignore extraneous information. In this strategy the teacher vocalizes his or her cognitive processes, or thoughts. While going through a text, the teacher says aloud what he or she is thinking about the main ideas and supporting details. For example, in reading a paragraph on national parks, the teacher might model the think-aloud strategy by saying:

> *As I read the heading of the paragraph, I am alert to the fact that this piece of writing seems to be about national parks. As I continue to look at the page, I see a picture of a man who developed the idea of preserving national parkland. I notice a chart that gives dates when each national park was established. This paragraph seems to be about the early development of national parks. Let's read it to see if that's so . . . .*

Main Idea and Supporting Details

Communicating Main Ideas

It is imperative that secondary level students communicate main ideas. One strategy is to have students read a short piece of text and then work in groups to identify the main idea. After identifying the main idea, each group writes it on a sentence strip and shares it with the class. When they have mastered this skill, they will be able to synthesize key information whenever they are listening and/or reading and articulate the main idea, key concept, or central theme.

Communicating Critical Details

In addition to communicating the main idea, students must be able to communicate the critical details that support it. Main idea and supporting details are a mental construct that students must internalize. Have students analyze and synthesize text information. Show them how analyzing requires them to break the information into details that connect to the main idea. Then show them how synthesizing requires them to connect all of the details by forming a generalization. Have students share their analyses and syntheses frequently in class with partners, small groups, and the whole class in order to gain proficiency.

Main Idea and Supporting Details

Using Strategies Independently

The goal of all strategy instruction is that students will be able to select and use strategies independently to meet their needs as readers. Model the strategies included in this section (and in all sections that follow); and when students are ready, allow them to work in groups and with partners to determine the main idea. After diagnosing their proficiency in determining the main idea, allow students to engage in guided practice with independent reading activities that require them to identify the main idea and supporting details. Expose students to a variety of texts in terms of topic, readability, and complexity of ideas presented.

Strategy 1: SQ3R

Survey, question, read, recite, and review (SQ3R) (Robinson, 1970, as described in Irvin, 1998) is an excellent strategy for helping students determine the main idea.

- ✓ Begin by having students **survey** the text for organizational structure. Give them a few minutes to look through the chapter noting the heading and subheadings and looking for introductory and summary paragraphs, boldface type, margin notes, captions, graphs, photos, and illustrations. Research has shown that when students have a strong and accurate awareness of structure, they are better able to determine and retain main ideas and supporting details.
- ✓ Next, have students convert subheadings into **questions** and find answers as they read. For example, if a chapter subheading is "Similarities Between Frogs and Toads," students should convert it to a question: What are the similarities between frogs and toads?
- ✓ After forming their questions, students then **read** one section at a time looking for answers to the questions they asked.
- ✓ Next, pair students with partners and have them **recite** (or write) a key phrase, summary, or paraphrase of the important information they read by referring to the answers that they generated.
- ✓ In the **review** stage, have students use graphic organizers or a list of key phrases to reformulate their knowledge for a deeper understanding and to test themselves on what they recall about the chapter.

If you use this method, do it often enough to make it second nature for students. For this strategy to be effective, students should be able to do the steps without having to think about them.

Main Idea and Supporting Details

Strategy 2: Finding the Main Idea and Supporting Details

To use this four-step strategy, begin with a paragraph in which the main idea is obvious, even if it is not stated in a topic sentence. The passage must be at students' independent reading levels. The following example of this strategy also helps students to understand that there is a difference between the topic of a passage and the main idea.

> The Berlin Wall, built by the Communists in 1961, split the country of Germany in two. People on the east side of the wall could no longer go to West Germany; people on the west side could no longer go to East Germany. The wall was 20 feet high and made of solid concrete with barbed wire along the top. Soldiers, dogs, and guards in watchtowers kept people from crossing over the wall.

Step 1: Identify the key word(s) in each sentence.

1. Berlin Wall, Communists, Germany
2. people on east side
3. people on west side
4. high, concrete, barbed wire
5. soldiers, dogs, watchtowers

Step 2: Identify the topic (what all the sentences have in common).

The Berlin Wall

Step 3: Write a sentence stating the main idea (based on information from Steps 1 and 2).

The Berlin Wall split Germany and kept apart the people on both sides.

Step 4: If possible, locate a sentence in the paragraph that states the main idea.

"The Berlin Wall, built by the Communists in 1961, split the country of Germany in two."

The Main Idea and Supporting Details worksheet on page 17 also helps students determine the main idea and evaluate the importance of details.

Strategy 3: Examining Graphic Features

To understand the structure of nonfiction, students need to be familiar with the use of graphic elements that can help them discover the main idea and supporting details. The worksheet on page 15 helps them use titles, headings, subheadings, charts, graphs, pictures, and illustrations to discover the main idea.

Main Idea and Supporting Details

Strategy 4: Previewing the Text to Make Predictions

Another strategy that helps students to use graphic features to determine the main idea is to have them preview the chapter and make predictions about what will be important and what might not be. The worksheet on page 18 provides practice in this strategy.

Strategy 5: A Self-Monitoring Approach to Reading and Thinking (SMART)

Developed by Vaughn and Estes (1986) and further described by Irvin (1998), this simple five-step strategy helps students discover what they don't understand in the text.

Step 1: Do I understand?

Students read a paragraph and ask,"Do I totally understand everything in this paragraph?" They place a check in the margin of the text or on a sticky note when they understand and a question mark when they do not.

Step 2: What have I just read?

At the end of each paragraph, students stop to summarize in their own words what they have just read. They can look back at the text during this activity.

Step 3: Does it make sense now?

After students finish reading the text, they return to each paragraph that has a question mark and reread. If it still does not make sense, they move to step 4.

Step 4: Why am I having this trouble?

Students try to pinpoint the problem. Is the difficulty unfamiliar words or concepts? Is the sentence structure too complex? Do they have little background information about the topic? Students need to figure out their specific stumbling blocks before moving to step 5.

Step 5: Where can I get help?

Students should try a variety of aids: glossary, appendix, dictionary, chapter summary, etc. If they are still confused after going through these five steps, they need to ask a classmate or teacher for assistance.

As students become more comfortable with this strategy, make a rule that they cannot ask for help from the teacher unless they can do the following:

- Identify the exact source of their confusion.
- Describe the steps they've already taken on their own to resolve the problem.

Main Idea and Supporting Details

Strategy 6: Text Coding

When secondary level students use text coding, they are able to monitor their understanding as they read. Provide students with the following codes:

I = Important

MI = Main Idea or Connects to Main Idea

SD = Supporting Detail

Q = Question

As they read, have them mark the text directly or use sticky notes to record the appropriate codes. When they have finished reading, have them use the double-entry journal format to record the words and phrases that correspond with the codes. In the response column, have students identify why the information is important, how the text connects to the main idea, or questions that they have about the text. Use the Text Coding and Main Idea worksheet (page 19) for this strategy.

Strategy 7: Box Webs

Using art strategies to represent the main idea and supporting details can be highly motivating especially to struggling readers. Have them use the Box Web worksheet (page 20) to draw their illustrations of the main idea and four supporting details and to explain how engaging in this activity helps them to understand the text information.

Strategy 8: Personal Experience and Prior Knowledge

Connecting to personal experience and prior knowledge is a good way to motivate students to find supporting details and retain the information once they have found it. Use the worksheets (pages 21 and 22) to provide a framework for students to identify the supporting details on the left side of the chart. Then students respond in a variety of ways by connecting the text to their life experiences or to their prior knowledge of the topic or concept on the right side of the chart.

Strategy 9: Novelty Notetaking

A simple but powerful notetaking technique is to have students use a two-column format (page 23) to record facts from the text on the left side and then reflect on how those facts connect to the main idea on the right side of the journal. After students complete this activity, have them work with a partner to compare the right side of the journal and to discuss the similarities and differences among the connections that they made.

Main Idea and Supporting Details

Strategy 10: Retelling and Reacting

Retelling is a critical component to identifying the main idea and supporting details. Provide students with the Retelling and Reacting worksheet (page 24) and have them restate in their own words the important events in the text on the left side of the chart. Then have them react on the right side of the chart by identifying how the retold events connect to their own lives, reveal the main idea, or provide information that is important to know. Allow students the opportunity to deduce the main idea by re-examining the chart.

Strategy 11: Tic-Tac-Toe and Details

Give students a blank Tic-Tac-Toe worksheet (page 25) and have them read text and fill in the details from the text. Then have them switch papers with a partner and give them tokens. Have partners read the text. Every time they find one of the details from the game card, instruct them to place a token (page 26) on the appropriate box. The first person to place three tokens in a row horizontally, vertically, or diagonally wins. Close by having students complete Part C.

Examining Graphic Features

Directions: Examine the graphic features of the text and determine the main idea.

Chapter or section title: ______________________________

Headings and subheadings: ______________________________

____

____

____

Graphic features (charts, graphs, pictures, etc.):

Identify	Describe
1.	
2.	
3.	

Based on your examination of the graphic features, what is the main idea? Write the main idea in your own words.

____

____

____

How did examining the graphic features help you identify the main idea?

____

____

____

Main Idea and Supporting Details

Directions: Identify the main idea and supporting details. Make sure to evaluate the importance of the supporting details.

Concept or topic being studied: ______________________________

Title of the text: ______________________________

Main Idea: ______________________________

Identify three supporting details and rate their importance in understanding the main idea.

1 = Very Important
2 = Somewhat Important
3 = Not Very Important

Supporting Details	Importance Rating
1.	
2.	
3.	

Do the supporting details help you to better understand the topic that you are studying? Explain.

____

____

____

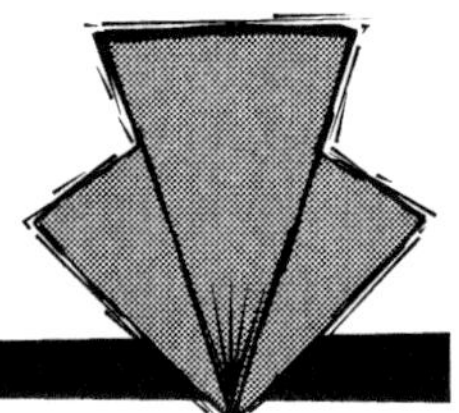

Previewing the Text to Make Predictions

Directions: Answer the following questions to determine the main idea.

What is the text length and structure?	What are the important headings and subheadings?
What should I be sure to read and in what order should I read it?	What parts of the text should I read very carefully?
What parts of the text do not look important? What should I skip or ignore?	How will the text connect to my prior knowledge?

What is the main idea? ______________________________

How do I know? ______________________________

____

____

____

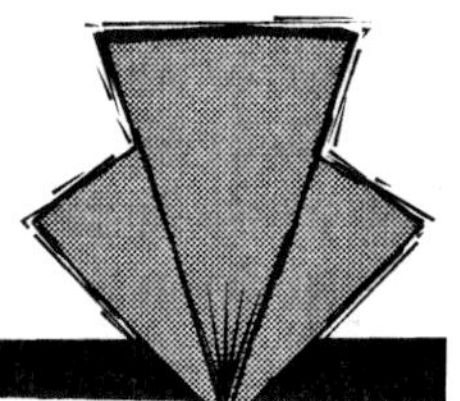

Text Coding and Main Idea

Directions: As you read, use the following codes to mark on a sticky note next to words or phrases that reveal the main idea. Then use the chart below to record the words or phrases and to reflect on how they show the main idea or supporting details.

I = Important

MI = Main Idea or Connects to Main Idea

SD = Supporting Detail

Q = Question (This seems important, but I am not sure how. . . .

Words or Phrases that reveal Main Idea and Supporting Detail	**Response** (Choose from the sentence starters below to get you started on your response.) • This information is important because. . . • The text connects to the main idea because. . . • This supporting detail is important because. . . • I am not sure how this connects to the main idea but. . .

Box Web

Directions: Draw pictures of the main idea in the center box and four supporting details in the other boxes.

Supporting Detail	**Supporting Detail**
Main Idea	
Supporting Detail	**Supporting Detail**

How does illustrating the main idea and supporting details help you to understand the information?

____

____

____

Connecting the Main Idea and Supporting Details to Prior Knowledge

Directions: Connect the main idea and supporting details to your prior knowledge.

Main Idea	Prior Knowledge about the Main Idea

Supporting Detail 1:	Prior Knowledge or Questions:
Supporting Detail 2:	**Prior Knowledge or Questions:**
Supporting Detail 3:	**Prior Knowledge or Questions:**

How will connecting to your prior knowledge help you to remember main ideas and supporting details?

____

____

____

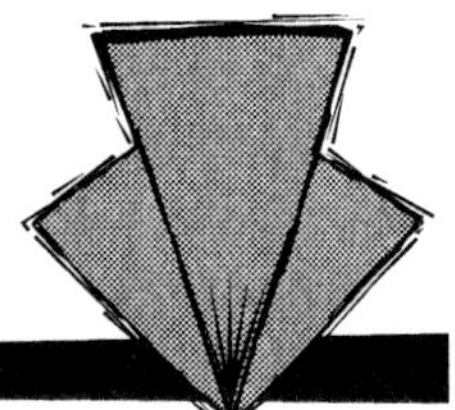

Responding to Supporting Details

Directions: Connect your own life to the main ideas and supporting details in the text by writing the main idea in the space provided. Then under the Supporting Details heading, write four details that support the main idea. In the response column answer all questions for each detail.

Main Idea____

Supporting Details	Response • How does this supporting detail connect to my life? • How does this supporting detail further explain the main idea? • How is this supporting detail important to me? Why will I need this information?

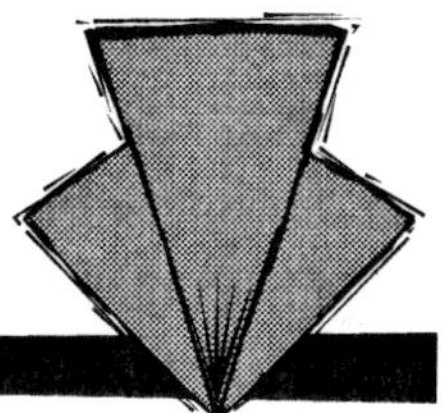

Novelty Notetaking

Directions: Record facts and details from the text in the left column. In the right column, react to each fact or detail by answering the following questions:

1. How do the details connect to the main idea?
2. Is the author's approach to the subject "novel" or unique? How?
3. What further questions do you have?

Facts and Details from the Text	Reactions

Retelling and Reacting

Directions: In the left column retell four important events or ideas from the text. In the right column react by answering the following questions for each event or idea:

How do these events or ideas relate to my life?

How do these events or ideas reveal the main idea?

Why are these events or ideas important for me to know?

Important Events/Ideas	Reactions

What is the main idea? ____

Tic-Tac-Toe and Details

Part A Directions: Read the text and place one detail in each of the boxes below.

Part B Directions: Switch papers with a partner. Read the text, and use the tokens on page 35 to cover a detail every time you find one written on the paper. The first one to place three tokens in a row horizontally, vertically, or diagonally wins.

Part C Directions: Use the details to make a generalization about the main idea of the article. Write your information on the back of this paper.

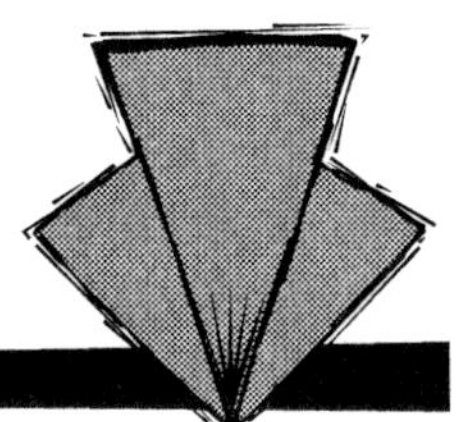

Tic-Tac-Toe and Details *(cont.)*

Directions: Cut out the tokens for use with the Tic-Tac-Toe activity on page 33.

Token	Token	Token
Token	Token	Token
Token	Token	Token

Summarizing and Paraphrasing

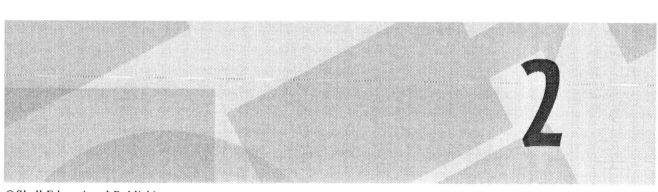

Summarizing and Paraphrasing

Introduction

Once students have attempted or mastered the ability to find the main idea and supporting details, they are ready to learn to summarize and paraphrase the nonfiction material that they read. Summarizing and paraphrasing require the development and use of a variety of skills. First, both require that students use critical thinking strategies because they must be able to understand the content of what they read and also extract the essential elements of a passage. Then, they must express the content in a way that is understandable to themselves and to their readers.

Second, paraphrasing requires that students use vocabulary skills. In order to paraphrase material, they must understand crucial words. They also must have a good grasp of synonyms or know where to find them. Additionally, they need to use what they know about syntax, or sentence structure, to rewrite an author's sentences in new ways that avoid plagiarism.

Summarizing materials can help students with retention of information. The skill of summarizing can also be used to understand the argument that an author is trying to make or to compare and contrast points of view either within a single piece or between two pieces of writing. It can also help students grasp complicated scientific processes or social movements as they pull together a collection of thoughts.

What Is Summarizing?

Summarizing briefly recounts the important points in a piece of text. Both fiction and nonfiction can be summarized, but for the purposes of this book, only summarizing as it pertains to nonfiction will be addressed. The basic steps of a summary are to think about the main idea or message of the text and then to recall the most important ideas that the author made in the text using a web, note cards, or bullets. Finally, the summary is written. Unless there is a specific reason to include an author's opinion, an important requirement of a summary is that it is based only on facts. In this way the reader can draw his or her own conclusion based on the facts presented.

Summarizing and Paraphrasing

What Is Paraphrasing?

Paraphrasing is the act of putting someone else's words into one's own words. Although the ideas may come from someone else, paraphrasing allows a writer to repeat the ideas in an original way in his or her own style. Paraphrasing is not the same as quoting the source material in its initial form. In fact, paraphrasing can be better than quoting, especially when a passage is not particularly noteworthy or well written. For this reason, students need to use many synonyms and transitional words to help them paraphrase material effectively.

Being able to restate information in one's own words is a critical skill. Begin by having students preview the text for important information. As they read, have them take notes about information related to the topics or concepts they are studying. Finally, have them put their notes away and restate the most important information in their own words.

Selecting Significant Text Information

After students preview the text and delve into the reading, it is essential that they know how to recognize important information. Remind them to pay particular attention to the following text features:

- headings and subheadings
- bolded words
- italicized words
- captions
- illustrations
- photographs
- charts
- graphs
- maps
- labels

Model how to ask questions in order to identify significant text information. The following questions will help students focus on the text:

- What are the key concepts and/or main ideas?
- What are the important facts?
- How does the information I am reading connect to what I am learning in class?
- How do the text features help me to understand what's significant?

Summarizing and Paraphrasing

Preserving the Author's Perspective

In order to preserve the author's perspective when summarizing or paraphrasing, it is important to identify what that point of view is. Use the following questions to guide discussions:

- What is the author's perspective, or point of view, on the topic?
- How can I tell the author's perspective? Is it implicit or explicit?
- What valuable information have I learned by preserving the author's perspective, or point of view?

Organizing Information

There are many ways for students to organize the information that they encounter. Some of the more traditional approaches include outlining and using note cards. It is important to teach students how to use traditional approaches, but it is also important to show them various techniques to allow for the diverse learning styles in your classroom. Some of these techniques include graphic organizers, such as double-entry journals. Given the amount of information with which students will interact over the course of their education, it is essential that they have various tools to sort information into key concepts, main ideas, and supporting details in order to summarize and paraphrase.

Using Strategies

Extensive teacher modeling of the following strategies will help students understand how to summarize and paraphrase. All strategies should be done as a whole group and then with a partner several times before letting students work independently. Be sure to model strategies in a variety of content areas, including math.

Strategy 1: Summarizing Through Drawing

To get students started with the skill of summarizing, give them the definition of summarizing: relating the most important information to a given audience. Read students a short piece of nonfiction and tell them to think about the most important information. Then give students a blank sheet of paper and have them draw a picture of the key ideas in the text. Tell them that they can be as creative as they want and that they can use captions or labels, but they are not to write a paragraph. When they are finished, have them share their artistic creations with the class. On the overhead or board, keep track of students' ideas and look for commonalities among their understandings of what is most important.

Summarizing and Paraphrasing

Strategy 2: Writing Summaries

Writing summaries requires critical thinking. Students first need to figure out the main idea and the supporting details. Then they must condense the author's ideas. Finally, they must be concise, writing as much information as the reader needs in as few words and sentences as possible. Select a nonfiction paragraph or section of a class textbook and use the following steps to teach summary writing:

Step 1: Read the Material

Tell students to read carefully the material to be summarized. They should think about the author's main idea as they read. What ideas does the author return to repeatedly?

Step 2: Reread the Material and Make Notes

Skim the material quickly. Students may jot down key words and phrases on a separate sheet of paper. If the text is long, they may wish to have a separate note card for each section that they will be summarizing.

Step 3: Put the Material Aside

Direct students to close the article or textbook and begin thinking about how they want to summarize the author's ideas. They should write the author's main idea in a sentence or two and then look over their notes for information they wish to include. They can expand the notes they have made into complete sentences.

Step 4: Write the Summary

Next, students are to organize their expanded sentences into a summary. Summaries may be as brief as three sentences or as long as a page, depending on the length of the article, chapter, or book that they read. They can use the main idea to guide their organization. They might also want to think about the type of text they read. Is it a description? Does it cover a chronological period? In addition, certain transitional words, such as "in addition," "as a result," "however," "for example, "first," "later," "also," can help them tie together the ideas contained in their summary.

Step 5: Check Your Work

Have students look over their completed summaries. Then return to the original material. Did they capture what the author was trying to say? Is there any information that was left out or that is not needed? Ask students to rewrite their summaries as needed.

After you have them practice summarizing a passage, distribute page 38, which gives them a seven-step plan for writing a summary. Students can keep it to use as a reference.

Strategy 3: Outlining

Outlines help students organize their notes and portray hierarchical relationships. To help students understand how an outline relates to expository text, provide a nonfiction passage with the important words and phrases at the bottom of the page. Provide a second page with the appropriate Roman numerals, capital letters, and Arabic numbers. Then read the passage and complete the outline as a whole group or have students work in pairs. The following example on Komodo dragons can be used for this activity:

Komodo Dragons

Komodo dragons are one of the world's scariest animals. They are the biggest lizards in the world and grow to be 10 feet (3 m) long, and can weigh up to 300 pounds (136 kg). Their bodies have thick, dark scales that look like a knight's armor. They have sharp, jagged teeth, and claws the length of a human adult's longest finger. Dragons flick their forked tongue to smell for prey.

Besides looking terrifying, Komodo dragons are good hunters. They can run up to 10 miles per hour (16 kph) to get their prey. Then they unhinge their jaws so they can swallow pieces of meat that are bigger than their own heads. This lets them eat really big animals such as deer, wild pigs, cattle, and water buffalo. They will also eat any human being they can catch.

Komodo dragons live in burrows. They also dig deep holes in the ground to bury about two dozen eggs. After eight months the baby dragons hatch and dig themselves out of their nest. They must hide from adult dragons, including their parents, who will eat them. The babies soon learn to stay up in trees and come down only to eat. Their food is the scraps left after all the adults have finished eating.

Komodo dragons live only on Komodo Island, located between Australia and Southeast Asia. Today they are endangered because humans have wiped out much of their prey.

Important Words/Phrases

appearance
weigh up to 300 pounds
bodies
prey
thick, dark scales
run up to 10 miles per hour
eat leftovers from adult kills
Komodo dragons today
for homes
hide in treetops

biggest lizards in the world
hunting
getting food
unhinge jaws to swallow big pieces
long claws
deer
wild pigs
cattle
avoid adults
endangered due to humans

grow to be 10 feet long
sharp, jagged teeth
water buffalo
forked tongue
baby dragons
reproduction
livc only on Komodo Island
burrows
for eggs

Summarizing and Paraphrasing

An outline for the passage might look like the following:

Komodo Dragons

I. Appearance
  A. Biggest lizards in the world
    1. grow to 10 feet long
    2. weigh up to 300 pounds
  B. Bodies
    1. thick, dark scales
    2. sharp, jagged teeth
    3. long claws
    4. forked tongue

II. Hunting
  A. Getting food
    1. run up to 10 miles per hour
    2. unhinge jaws to swallow big pieces
  B. Prey
    1. deer
    2. wild pigs
    3. cattle
    4. water buffalo

III. Reproduction
  A. Burrows
    1. for homes
    2. for eggs
  B. Baby Dragons
    1. avoid adults
    2. hide in treetops
    3. eat leftovers from adult kills

IV. Komodo dragons today
  A. live only on Komodo Island
  B. endangered due to humans

Summarizing and Paraphrasing

Strategy 4: Summary Frame

A summary frame can help students write a personalized summary. Provide students with copies of a summary frame. Have them write their individual responses after the "knew" statement. Next, have them read the text and then complete the frame. For example:

Before I started reading about the Black Plague, I knew it was a fatal disease that had killed much of the European population. People knew little about germs or sanitary conditions.

In the article I learned that <u>the Plague occurred during 1347–1351 and killed 50,000 people in Paris alone. Nobody knows the exact death toll because records weren't kept, but an estimated one third of Europe's whole population perished.</u>

I also learned <u>it was caused by a germ carried by the fleas that lived on rats.</u>

I was surprised <u>to find out that right before the Plague began people had killed off most of the cats, believing that they were satanic. Since the cats had kept the rat population in check, this meant that there were more rats than ever. If there had only been more cats, the Plague would not have been as bad.</u>

Use the template on page 40 for practice in summary frames.

Strategy 5: 5 W's + H

The 5 W's + H strategy can help students focus on what is important. Students can use the double-entry journal for 5 W's + H (page 41) to record key information from the text and to write a summary using this information. Another way to have students use this strategy is to divide them into groups of four to six and assign each member of the group one of the 5 W's + H. This variation forces them to focus on one element of the text as they are reading. Have them fill out a graphic organizer together when they are finished reading and share their information.

When? **How?** **Why?**

What? **Who?** **Where?**

Summarizing and Paraphrasing

Strategy 6: Key Word Notetaking

Key word notetaking (page 42) is a way for students to read for important information, create a study guide, and practice summarizing at the same time. Students record key words (sometimes with a verb) on the left side of the notetaking form. Then on the right side, they convert the key word(s) into a statement. Model how to make these statements from a passage or article. After students have completed this graphic organizer, show them how to use it as a study guide. Model how to fold the graphic organizer on the line that divides the left side from the right side. Have students quiz themselves on the summaries that match the key words. Then show them how to turn the study guide over and quiz themselves on the key words that match the summaries. Students can work independently or with a partner to study this information. One of the benefits of this technique is that it builds the students' independence in mastering their own learning. The following example from a chapter in a textbook demonstrates this strategy:

Chapter 16: Pollution

pollution is (page 41)	Pollution is damage done to the earth created by waste. Pollution can hurt plants, animals, and humans.
pollution affects (page 42)	Pollution affects land, air, or water.
types of pollution (pages 41–43)	There are five kinds of pollution: • solid waste (trash, litter, junk) • air pollution (gases, smoke, chemicals, acid rain) • land pollution (chemicals, nuclear waste, solid waste) • water pollution (heat, chemicals, solid waste) • noise pollution (lots of loud sounds)
global warming (page 44)	Global warming means that the earth is warming up because there's too much carbon dioxide in the atmosphere. The carbon dioxide comes from cars, homes, and factories that burn gas, oil, and coal.

Summarizing and Paraphrasing

Strategy 7: Topic and Detail Summary Writing

Another graphic organizer that helps students to summarize is on page 43. This activity causes them to identify the topic and the important details and then use that information to write a short summary.

Strategy 8: Step-by-Step Paraphrasing

Paraphrasing, or rewriting material using other words, is a skill that requires modeling by the teacher and extensive practicing by students. To begin teaching paraphrasing, use the Paraphrasing worksheet on page 44, which takes students through the steps of the process by focusing on one sentence. The worksheet on page 45 explains the rules for paraphrasing—what to do and what not to do.

Strategy 9: Paraphrasing and Vocabulary

Paraphrasing requires students to understand crucial words, have a knowledge of synonyms, and use a thesaurus. Two worksheets—Paraphrasing with New Vocabulary (page 46) and Using a Thesaurus (page 47)—can help them understand the importance of knowing the meanings of words.

Strategy 10: Practice with Paraphrasing

Students need to practice the difficult skill of paraphrasing. The Practice with Paraphrasing worksheet on page 48 takes common proverbs and asks students to rewrite them in their own words while keeping the meanings intact. You might want to model how to paraphrase by doing the first one or two or have the whole group do the first two together.

Strategy 11: Paraphrase Passport

This strategy will help students develop their listening skills as well as their paraphrasing skills. Pair each student with a partner. One partner asks a question. Partner two answers the question. Partner one restates in his or her own words partner two's answer. Partner two agrees if his or her answer has been correctly answered. The partners switch roles. Here are some sentence starters to help with the paraphrasing:

> *Let me see if I understand what you are saying. . .*
>
> *If I hear you correctly, you are identifying. . .*
>
> *What you are telling me is. . .*

How to Write a Summary

A summary is a condensed, or short, version of a paragraph, chapter, article, or book. Summaries can serve several purposes. They can simply retell descriptive or chronological information or give a brief rundown of a process. They also can give an overview of an author's argument with the author's main idea and important points.

When you write a summary, you will need to do quite a bit of thinking. You will need to think about the author's main idea and the supporting details. You will also need to know how to paraphrase, or rewrite, the author's words in as brief a form as possible.

Summaries can be as short as a sentence or as long as a page or two, depending on the length of the material that you need to summarize.

Here are the seven steps to writing a summary:

Step 1: Read the material carefully.

Think about the main idea of what you are reading. Notice the most important supporting details or facts. Make sure that you understand the author's argument or conclusion.

Step 2: Reread the material.

As you read, think about the text type. Also, use the text organizers such as subheadings to help you organize your thinking about the material. You want to include information from each section of what you read. You may want to jot down any important points or key words and phrases that you would like to include in your summary.

Step 3: Write the main idea.

This will help you stay focused on the information to include in your summary.

Step 4: Write summary sentences.

Write down a sentence that tells about each section of what you read.

Step 5: Write a draft of your summary.

Look over the main idea, key words and phrases, and sentences that you wrote. Now write a summary that gives the basic information that the reader needs to know. You do not need to include all the supporting details in your summary. Just tell the reader a few of the most important facts.

Step 6: Check your information.

Look over the original material that you read. Did you include only the most important points? Did you leave out anything that the reader should know?

Step 7: Rewrite your summary.

Read your work. It should read smoothly. Add transitional words when necessary.

Outlining

Directions: Outline the passage or article you are reading. If you need more numbers or letters, use the back of this page.

Topic: ______________________________

I. ______________________________

  A. ______________________________

    1. ______________________________

    2. ______________________________

  B. ______________________________

    1. ______________________________

    2. ______________________________

II. ______________________________

  A. ______________________________

    1. ______________________________

    2. ______________________________

  B. ______________________________

    1. ______________________________

    2. ______________________________

III. ______________________________

  A. ______________________________

    1. ______________________________

    2. ______________________________

  B. ______________________________

    1. ______________________________

    2. ______________________________

IV. ______________________________

  A. ______________________________

    1. ______________________________

    2. ______________________________

  B. ______________________________

    1. ______________________________

    2. ______________________________

Summary Frame

Directions: Before you begin reading, fill in the first frame. After reading, fill in the other frames.

Before I started reading about ____________, I knew ______________________________________

____

____

____

In the article, I learned ____

____

____

____

____

____

I also learned____

____

____

____

I was surprised that____

____

____

____

____

____

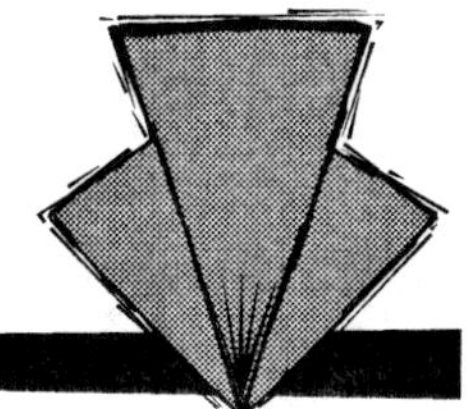

Using the 5 W s + H

Directions: Read the text and identify the 5 W's + H on the left side of the double-entry journal. Then write a summary on the right side.

5 W's + H	Summary of 5 W's + H
Who:	
What:	
Where:	
When:	
Why:	
How:	

Key Word Notetaking

Directions: Record key words with page numbers in the left column. In the right column, convert the key words into two statements.

Topic: ______________________________

Key Words & Page #	Statements
	1. 2.
	1. 2.
	1. 2.
	1. 2.

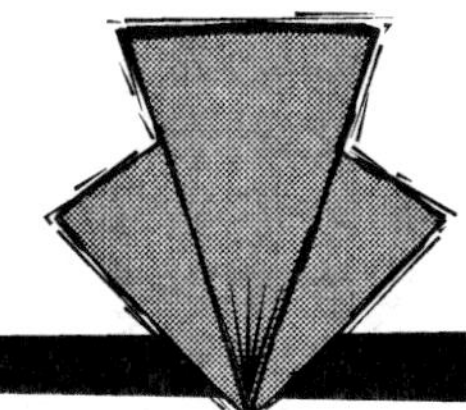

Topic and Detail Summary Writing

Directions: Identify the topic and the details from the text and then use the information to write a summary.

Topic:
Important Details 1. 2. 3.

Summary Directions: Use the information above to write a summary that clearly does the following:

- includes the important facts in your own words
- combines facts where possible
- excludes extraneous information

Paraphrasing

To paraphrase means to rewrite material in either another form or other words. Paraphrasing is a useful skill for several reasons. You can use it when you write reports and need to retell facts. Paraphrasing prevents you from plagiarizing or stealing someone else's words. Also, when you are able to paraphrase words, you show that you understand the idea or meaning of what you have read.

Directions: Complete the following steps in paraphrasing.

1. Be sure that you understand all of the vocabulary words in the material that you are going to paraphrase. For example, read the following sentence:

   Eleanor Roosevelt was a true humanitarian and a friend to the poor and oppressed.

   Do you know the meaning of the words "humanitarian" and "oppressed"? Define the words on the lines below.

   humanitarian: ______________________________

   oppressed: ______________________________

2. Think about the important parts of the sentence—the subject, verb, and object. Write these on the lines below.

   subject: ______________________________

   verb: ______________________________

   object: ______________________________

3. Now think about some synonyms for the words "humanitarian" and "oppressed."

   synonyms for humanitarian: ______________________________

   synonyms for oppressed: ______________________________

4. There are also phrases in a sentence to be avoided when paraphrasing. For example, even if you find a synonym for "humanitarian," you would not want to use the adjective "true" in front of it. Do you see another phrase to avoid? Write it below.

   ____

5. Finally, paraphrase the sentence about Eleanor Roosevelt in your own words using your synonyms and new language.

   ____

Extension: Can you think of two additional ways to paraphrase the sentence?

____

____

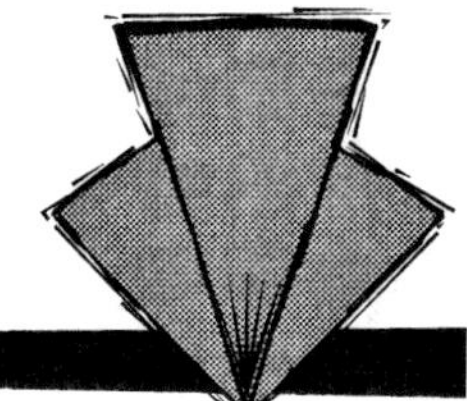

Do s and Don ts of Paraphrasing

Many students wrongly believe that they can just substitute a word or two in a sentence in order to paraphrase it. The problem in substituting is that it still causes plagiarism, or the stealing of someone else's words. In order to paraphrase correctly, follow these guidelines.

- Do think of or look up synonyms for as many words as you can, not just unusual ones.
- Do change the order of the wording in the sentence.
- Do put aside the work you are paraphrasing so you are not tempted to copy it.
- Do write the paraphrase a few different ways and choose the best one.
- Do copy the original sentence or sentences onto separate paper and then edit them with proofreader's marks in order to change their meaning.

Follow these important "Don'ts" as well.

- Don't change the meaning of the original sentence or paragraph because you did not understand it.
- Don't add your own ideas to the author's or change the author's ideas.
- Don't use synonyms that do not quite fit the author's meaning.
- Don't say more or less than the author meant to say.

Directions: Now try writing the following sentences in two or three different ways. Look up any vocabulary about which you are unclear. Use synonyms that you either know or need to look up in a thesaurus. Remember to think about the author's meaning.

1. Many arctic animals survive winter by burying themselves in the ground before it freezes.

____

____

____

2. Moose and deer spend the day grazing in the coniferous forest.

____

____

3. Since food for animals is abundant in the deciduous forest, there is also an abundance of animal life.

____

____

____

Paraphrasing with New Vocabulary

Directions: In order to be able to paraphrase a sentence or paragraph, you must understand any new vocabulary words that you find. Sometimes, too, when you understand all vocabulary words in the sentence, it becomes a much easier task to rewrite it. Each of the sentences below has difficult vocabulary in it for you to define. Then, after defining the words, rewrite the sentence so that it still makes sense. Use a separate sheet of paper for your work.

1. It wasn't until the 1880s that scientists recognized that the study of fossilized animal life could trace the evolutionary history of extinct species.

   Vocabulary words: fossilized, evolutionary, extinct, species

2. All dinosaurs walked with an erect posture unlike that of reptiles.

   Vocabulary words: erect, posture

3. Fossils are formed when an organism is buried in mud or sand before the hard parts of its body decay.

   Vocabulary words: organism, decay

4. Like the giant dragonfly, all invertebrate animals grew very large in prehistoric times.

   Vocabulary words: invertebrate, prehistoric

5. There are several rudimentary differences between endothermic and ectothermic animals.

   Vocabulary words: rudimentary, endothermic, ectothermic

6. Some reptiles have skin that changes due to fear, as well as fluctuations in light, humidity, and temperature.

   Vocabulary words: fluctuations, humidity

7. Due to its scarcity, an albino snake can command as much as $20,000 for its owner.

   Vocabulary words: scarcity, albino, command

8. Herpetologists conduct their studies in many different habitats.

   Vocabulary words: herpetologist, conduct, habitats

9. In spite of the extreme conditions in the desert, animal life is abundant and varied.

   Vocabulary words: extreme, abundant, varied

10. A reptile's scales act as a moisture barrier to prevent the reptile from dehydrating.

    Vocabulary words: barrier, dehydrating

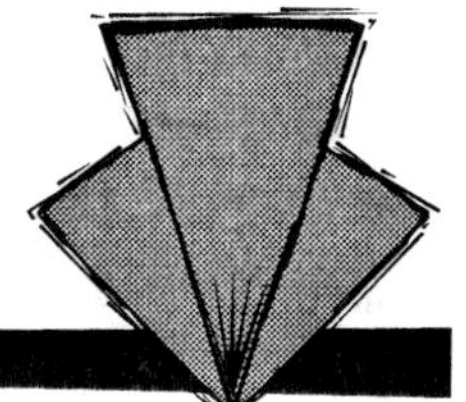

Using a Thesaurus

A thesaurus is a book of synonyms. Several different thesauruses are published, and some are more user-friendly than others. At the bottom of this sheet, you will even find some resources for thesauruses on the Internet. A thesaurus can be especially helpful when you are trying to paraphrase someone else's work. It can help you express the new ideas you have learned from your nonfiction reading in your own way.

There are some disadvantages to using a thesaurus. One is that you can come to depend on it. When you need to substitute a word, first try to think of a new word on your own. Another problem is that you need to pick words from the thesaurus that sound like you. Try to choose words that you would naturally use; otherwise, the word may stand out from the rest of your work and stop your reader's flow of thought.

Directions: Look up the following words in a thesaurus. Then write a sentence using one of the synonyms that you found on a separate sheet of paper.

1. dark: ____________________
2. follow: ____________________
3. sad: ____________________
4. nice: ____________________
5. polite: ____________________
6. dry: ____________________
7. brittle: ____________________
8. scary: ____________________
9. fearful: ____________________
10. tame: ____________________
11. brave: ____________________
12. small: ____________________

Internet Resources

http://thesaurus.reference.com: This site is an online version of *Roget's Thesaurus.*

http://www.m-w.com/dictionary.htm: Here is the *Merriam Webster* online edition of the *Collegiate Thesaurus.*

http://www.wordsmyth.net/home.php: This site is a complete dictionary that includes synonyms.

Practice with Paraphrasing

Directions: Read each proverb below and discuss its meaning with your classmates. Then paraphrase the proverbs. Paraphrasing proverbs and sayings can provide good practice to learn this skill. Remember that to *paraphrase* means to rewrite another author's words in your own words while still keeping the author's meaning.

1. A penny saved is a penny earned. ____________________
2. You can catch more flies with honey than with vinegar. ____________________

   ____
3. The only things certain in life are death and taxes. ____________________

   ____
4. Finders, keepers; losers, weepers. ____________________
5. Make hay while the sun shines. ____________________
6. Birds of a feather flock together. ____________________
7. Let sleeping dogs lie. ____________________
8. All's well that ends well. ____________________
9. Don't count your chickens before they hatch. ____________________
10. Haste makes waste. ____________________
11. An apple a day keeps the doctor away. ____________________
12. Great minds think alike. ____________________
13. Too many cooks spoil the broth. ____________________
14. A watched pot never boils. ____________________
15. A stitch in time saves nine. ____________________
16. Loose lips sink ships. ____________________
17. A journey of a thousand miles begins with a single step. ____________________

    ____
18. You can lead a horse to water, but you can't make it drink. ____________________

    ____
19. Home is where the heart is. ____________________
20. Beauty is in the eye of the beholder. ____________________

Developing Vocabulary

Developing Vocabulary

Introduction

Most teachers know that rote memorization of vocabulary words is ineffective for expanding students' word knowledge. Yet, students need to understand new words that they encounter in their reading if their knowledge base is to increase. In addition to learning word meanings in context, students also need skills to break down words in order to approach their reading with independence and confidence.

Nonfiction reading especially requires the ability to understand technical language. Science and social studies demand that students recognize and build their vocabulary. Mathematics also has a specialized language that students must learn if they are to advance.

Teaching vocabulary can be a frustrating experience if teachers do not have a plan other than assigning a list of words for students to define in the glossary or dictionary. Allot instructional time to word study. Students need to learn not only the meaning of words but also their applicability. In other words, once students learn a new term, they can think about other contexts in which the term might be used and in this way enlarge their understanding about that term. When beginning to read an interesting chapter or book, students are easily drawn into the material. Time spent on word study at the outset, however, will pay off handsomely as students will better comprehend the material and begin to use the vocabulary independently.

In short, Abbott (1999) states that vocabulary development should help students become adept at using a variety of word recognition strategies; unlock meanings of technical and specialized words in each content area; establish a systematic, lifelong method of vocabulary inquiry; and become motivated and enthusiastic about vocabulary study.

Selecting Vocabulary Words to Study

Many teachers feel overwhelmed when teaching vocabulary because they realize that it is impossible to cover thoroughly all the students' unknown words. Do not attempt to study every unknown word. Instead, choose words from each selection wisely. Following these guidelines will result in an educationally sound vocabulary list:

- First, choose words that are critical to the article's meaning.
- Then, choose conceptually difficult words.
- Finally, choose words with the greatest utility value—those that you anticipate students will see more often (e.g., choose "anxious" rather than "appalled").

If you prefer to give students a sense of control of their own learning, you can have them choose the words to be studied. First, put students into teams of three. Have them read the passage and decide as a group which three words they would like to study. When you reconvene as a class, each team tells you the three words it selected. Record their responses on the board, overhead, or chart paper. Do not record any word more than once. Once the list is established, have students define any terms that they can and look up the meaning of any others in the dictionary. Write the definition next to each term and have students copy all the information into their class notebooks.

Developing Vocabulary

Elements of Effective Vocabulary Instruction

A wide variety of techniques, as outlined in this section, is essential for successful vocabulary learning; and research has shown that the most effective vocabulary program utilizes contextual, structural, and classification strategies. Vocabulary instruction is only effective if students permanently add the concepts to their knowledge base. You can achieve success by making certain that your vocabulary instruction includes the following elements:

- Using context clues
- Knowing the meaning of affixes (prefixes, suffixes) and roots
- Learning synonyms and antonyms
- Categorizing (sorting) and classifying concepts

Using Context Clues

Learning vocabulary in context is important for two reasons. First, it makes students become active in determining word meanings; and second, it offers them a way to figure out unknown words in their independent reading. If you teach students how to use context clues, you will eventually be able to omit pre-teaching any vocabulary that is defined in context (as long as the text is written at students' independent reading levels).

There are five basic kinds of context clues:

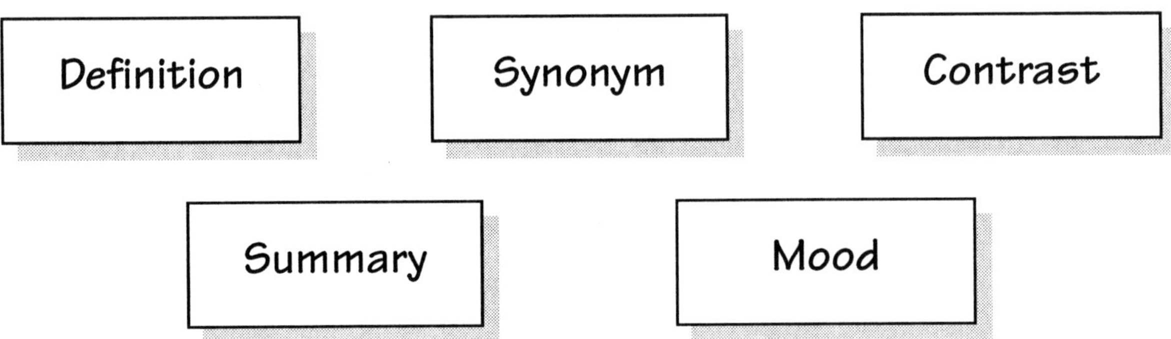

1. **Definition:** The easiest case occurs when the definition is given elsewhere in the sentence or paragraph.

   Example: The ragged, bedraggled dress hung from her shoulders.

Using Context Clues *(cont.)*

2. **Synonym:** Another simple case occurs when a synonym or synonymous phrase is immediately used.

   Example: The room was so dank that you could feel the dampness creep into your clothing.

3. **Contrast:** The meaning may be implied through contrast to a known word or concept. Be alert to these words that signal contrast: "although," "but," "however," "even though."

   Example: Clothes purchased off a department store rack will rarely be mistaken for haute couture.

4. **Summary:** Another form is a summary that provides a list of attributes.

   Example: Tundra, desert, grassland, and rain forest are the names of four of Earth's biomes.

5. **Mood:** Sometimes the meaning can be grasped from the mood of the larger context in which it appears. In the most difficult situation the meaning must be inferred with few other clues.

   Example: In America the end of World War II was marked by a wild sense of euphoria. People were singing and dancing in the streets, many businesses gave their workers the day off with pay, and almost every city nationwide had huge fireworks displays and parades.

   Example: Her shrill voice was actually making my ears hurt.

Words in Context

When students can define words in context, their comprehension levels will increase. Secondary school students should be proficient in using context to gain a clear sense of the concepts they are exploring, the topics they are studying, and the purpose for their learning. Structured discussions, small-group dialogues, and paired readings will build students' abilities to identify words in context because they will hear their teacher and classmates use unknown words in real-life conversations. When proficient readers encounter a word they don't know, they ask three questions:

- Do I know this word?
- If so, how do I know this word? If not, how can I know this word?
- Do I need to know this word?

Proficient readers answer these questions by using context, activating prior knowledge, and using resources available to them. Struggling readers have great difficulty using context and need highly structured word attack strategies in order to make sense of unknown words.

Developing Vocabulary

Word and Sentence Meanings

Students must be exposed to a variety of texts in all content areas. In each subject, students must be taught how to read sentences to determine word meaning. When using various techniques to make sense of words in context, students should consider the following word attack strategies:

1. Reread the sentence to try to understand the word based on sentence meaning.
2. Use the dictionary to find a definition that makes sense within the context of the sentence.
3. Reread the previous sentence.
4. Go on and read the next sentence.
5. Ask the teacher or a friend to read the sentence to you.
6. Look for key words in the sentence that may reveal the word's meaning.
7. Stop reading and think about what makes sense.
8. Look for pictures near the word or sentence to see if they help you understand.
9. Think about whether you need to know the word. Skip it if you don't.

Root Words

One of the main reasons for gains in vocabulary knowledge in students is their growing awareness and proficiency with root words, suffixes, and prefixes. *Morphology* is the ability to use word structures to make meaning of new vocabulary. Explicit instruction that teaches students how to use their prior knowledge to make sense of root words, suffixes, and prefixes will result in growing confidence in understanding words and ultimately an increase in reading comprehension. Some key questions will help students with using morphology.

1. What is the root word? What prior knowledge do I have to help me define this word?
2. What is the prefix? What does it mean? How does it change the root word?
3. What is the suffix? What does it mean? How does it change the root word?
4. How does knowing parts of words help me to understand the meaning of new words?

The worksheet on page 60 gives students practice in unlocking word meaning.

Developing Vocabulary

Interpreting Words with Multiple Meanings

Since many words have multiple meanings, students need to have ways to discern when a familiar word does not make sense in the context of the sentence. Often students will encounter a word being used differently because it has another definition with which they are unfamiliar. Words are also often used differently based on the subject area. For example, in math the word "change" means money. In science, "change" is connected to catalysts and experimentation. In social studies, "change" is connected to politics, history, and economics. A helpful technique to show the concept of multiple meanings is to create a large comparison chart that shows how words are used differently in each subject area. Make multiple copies of the chart so different content-area teachers can add to the chart during the school year, showing students how words are used differently across the content areas.

Identifying Shades of Meaning

When students are able to understand the shades of meaning of words, they will have deeper levels of comprehension. The ability to interpret different meanings of words is particularly useful when learning key concepts such as conflict, change, freedom, and symmetry. At the secondary school level, it is particularly beneficial for teachers to plan interdisciplinary lessons in which concepts and key vocabulary are discussed with particular attention paid to shades of meaning. Students will be able to make connections among major concepts and link facts to concepts when they explore multiple meanings.

Understanding Denotative and Connotative Meanings

By the time students are in secondary school, it is important for them to know the difference between denotative and connotative meanings. Remind them that denotative meaning is the dictionary definition of a word. Connotative meaning is the secondary implications or associated meanings of a word. Being able to connote meaning is a challenging task that requires the reader to understand the set of attributes that constitutes the meaning of a term.

Understanding Words Related to Content Areas

Students need to know the technical vocabulary for various content areas in order to better understand and acquire content knowledge. For example, in science, students should have mastery of certain words such as "experiment," "scientific method," "theory," "hypothesis," "catalyst," and "conclusion." Proficiency with such content-specific vocabulary will lead to greater facility with learning facts and increase students' abilities to synthesize and evaluate information.

Developing Vocabulary

Using Dictionaries and Other Reference Materials

While it is important to teach students how to identify the meanings of words in context and to use other text-based strategies, it is also important to give them continued practice with using dictionaries and other reference materials. Give them the opportunity to find word meanings by organizing individual and group games, such as scavenger hunts. Assign students content-specific vocabulary and have them use the guide words at the top of the page to find the word. Then have them identify the word's is meaning, parts of speech, and root.

Using Vocabulary Strategies Independently

Modeling how to define words in context, activate prior knowledge, and use available resources will provide the foundation for students using vocabulary strategies independently. Remember to have students engage in whole-class discussion, small-group activities, and paired reading in order to gain a greater facility with vocabulary through structured instruction and socialization. Gradually release the responsibility for learning new vocabulary based on your assessment of their readiness and independence.

Strategy 1: Contextual Defining

Struggling readers may have difficulty using context clues so it is important that they are presented with highly structured approaches to making meaning of words through context. Use the Contextual Defining worksheet (page 61) to have them identify the unknown word, copy the sentence in which it is used, and write an explanation of the context. Then expose students to contextual understandings from the teacher and a partner. Also, have them create their own sentences using the word. All students will benefit from this process, but struggling readers will benefit most through the structured support of their teachers and their classmates. The following example shows how to use this strategy:

Vocabulary word: *dispute*

Context from the Text	**Context from the Teacher**
The driver had a *dispute* with the police officer after he was pulled over for speeding.	The restaurant customer had a *dispute* with the waiter when he charged the customer for something she did not order.
Context from You (the student)	**Context from a Partner**
My mom and dad had a *dispute* when we ran out of gas on the way to school.	I had a *dispute* with my friend when she wouldn't share the ball with me.

Dictionary definition: A *dispute* is a disagreement or argument.

Developing Vocabulary

Strategy 2: Charting Characteristics

Charting key characteristics is a good technique for identifying attributes related to a particular set of terms. The Charting Characteristics worksheet (page 62) will help with this process. For example, if students were studying mammals in a science class, they would record the mammals in the left-hand column (mice, gorillas, cats, dogs, sheep, elephants, etc.). Across the top of the chart they would record various characteristics, such as carnivorous, herbivorous, omnivorous, domestic, wild, friendly, not friendly, travels in packs, travels independently, etc. Students would read the information about the mammals and place a check in the box that corresponds with the particular characteristic that they had confirmed in the text.

Strategy 3: Personal Association Vocabulary Strategy

When students make sense of vocabulary words by applying them to their own lives, there is a greater likelihood that they will retain the definitions in their long-term memories. For this strategy, students identify the vocabulary word and draw a simple illustration or symbolic representation of the word. Then they list their personal associations with the word. For example, if the word is "triangulate," students may focus on the prefix "tri" and associate with tricycle, triatholon, tripod, and trident. They may notice that all of these words have something to do with the number three. After some discussion with a peer group or a partner over the meaning of the word, students may look up the word in a dictionary. Then have them generate a list of examples and non-examples of the word based on their personal experience. Use the Personal Association Vocabulary Strategy worksheet (page 63) for this strategy.

Strategy 4: Vocabulary Explorations Through Questioning

Model this strategy by identifying an unknown word and asking students four questions to help them reflect on using the word, connecting it to personal experience, teaching the word to someone else, and encountering the word again. Use the questions from the Vocabulary Explorations Through Questioning worksheet (page 64). Then distribute the worksheet and have students use it as they read the text. The following is an example of this strategy for the word "adjacent."

Unusual or Unknown Word: adjacent	
Questions Heard	**Responses**
How would you use this vocabulary word in your writing or everyday conversation?	My house is adjacent to a park.
How does this vocabulary word connect to your personal experience or prior knowledge?	I have heard my mom give directions to our house and use the word "adjacent" when she tells someone we live next to the park.
How would you teach this vocabulary word to someone else?	I would tell them it means "next to" or "beside something" and then give them examples.
Where would you expect to encounter this word in the future?	I might see the word "adjacent" when a location or direction of something is being described.

Developing Vocabulary

Strategy 5: Text Coding and Vocabulary

Tell students that they will be focusing on vocabulary in their reading. Present them with the following codes:

** = Important

? = I don't understand

?? = I wonder. . .

➡ = This word connects to the concept because. . .

These codes will help them to focus on important words, words they don't understand or wonder about, and words that connect with the concept they are studying. Have them write directly in the text or use sticky notes to record their codes. When they finish reading, they can use the Text Coding and Vocabulary worksheet (page 65) to record the vocabulary words that they coded and to reflect on the words' meanings by using the sentence starters.

Strategy 6: Capsule Vocabulary

Originally developed by Crist (1975) and further explained by Judith Irvin (1990), capsule vocabulary incorporates listening, speaking, reading, and writing into the process of learning new vocabulary. Begin by preparing a "capsule" of vocabulary words related to the topic. This capsule could be a real container that holds the words, or you could draw a large picture of a capsule on the board and "fill" it with the vocabulary words by writing them in the drawing. Next, engage students in an extended discussion in which you use the capsule vocabulary words to discuss the topic. Then have students use the Capsule Vocabulary worksheet (page 66) to record the words, have a group conversation using the words, listen to the teacher and record the words, write a mini-story or description using the words, and read the text recording the number of times those words appear.

Strategy 7: Personification Vocabulary

With this strategy, students define unknown vocabulary words and then personify those words. For example, if a student were to personify the word "lovely," he or she might write: "Lovely walks down the street carrying a bundle of roses while flipping her luxurious chestnut-colored hair over her shoulders." Or if a student were to personify the word "hideous," he or she might write: "Hideous likes to hide in old gnarled trees and growl loudly while picking his teeth and scratching his head covered with greasy black hair." Use the Personification Vocabulary worksheet on page 67 for this strategy.

Developing Vocabulary

Strategy 8: Exploring Content Vocabulary

When students are studying a complicated or difficult concept, they need to focus on those words that are particularly troublesome. An effective strategy requires them to focus on one word at a time, asking why they need to know the word, how it connects to other words, which is the most challenging word, and which word is difficult to pronounce. These questions help them identify specifically any problems comprehending the material. Also, the Exploring Content Vocabulary worksheet (page 68) can help teachers identify students' trouble spots for re-teaching.

Strategy 9: Dictionary Definitions

To give students practice in looking up words in the dictionary, use the Dictionary Definitions worksheet on page 69. To vary this process, you can assign specific difficult words that students will encounter in a lesson or a text, or you can give students a blank worksheet and have them choose their own list of unfamiliar words as they read. This strategy can be done by individuals, with partners, or by small groups.

Strategy 10: Dramatic and Artistic Definitions

To build students' understanding of new words, use drama. Divide students into groups or pairs to create a mini-skit or dramatic "photograph" illustrating their understanding of a word. If students created a dramatic photograph of the word "antagonistic," they would have a student with an angry look on his or her face, frozen in a position of preparing to punch someone. The other students would face the antagonistic student in frozen positions with terrified looks on their faces.

For an artistic variation, use the Artistic Interpretations worksheet (page 70) to have students identify a word, define it in context, and look it up in a dictionary. They draw an illustration of the word interacting with other ideas, people, places, or things. For example, if the word is "freedom," a student may draw a picture of a happy person holding the American flag, or the Statue of Liberty, or a bald eagle—all symbols of freedom in our country. Such a picture shows that the student understood cultural synonyms for the word "freedom."

Strategy 11: Vocabulary Baseball

Games are highly motivational to students. To set up vocabulary baseball, post a home base, first base, second base, and third base strategically around the classroom. Divide the class into two teams. In addition to 10 batters, each team can have a score keeper and coaches at every base. For the first team up at bat, "pitch" the vocabulary word to the first batter. The batter needs to define the word, use it in a sentence, and spell the word. For each part that the batter does correctly, he or she gets a base. For example, if the batter can do all three things, he or she has hit a triple. When a player cannot do any part, he or she is out. When the team has three outs, it sits down and the other team bats. If students have prepared for the game, you may not have many outs, so you may have to set a five-run limit.

Roots/Prefixes/Suffixes

Directions: Identify the unknown words. Look up and record the definitions, roots, prefixes, and

Unknown Word	Definition	Root	Prefixes	Suffixes

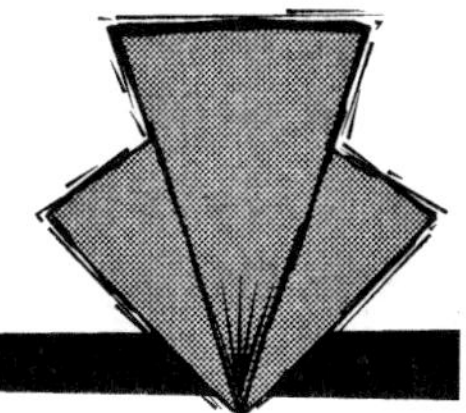

Contextual Defining

Directions: Use the following four contexts to come to an understanding of the unknown word.

Vocabulary word: ______________________________

Context from the Text Copy the sentence in which the word is found or explain the context.	**Context from the Teacher** Copy the sentence from the teacher in which the word is used in context.
Context from You Create a sentence in which you use the word in context based on the text's use and your teacher's use.	**Context from a Partner** Copy the sentence that your partner wrote in which he or she applied contextual understanding.

Dictionary definition: ______________________________

____

How did the contextual defining exercise help you to understand the word before you looked it up in the dictionary?

____

____

____

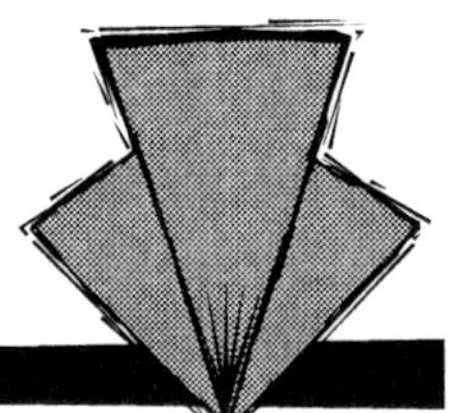

Charting Characteristics

Directions: Record terms to be compared and the characteristics that you will analyze. As you learn about each term, place a check in the characteristics column that connects to the term.

Characteristics to be analyzed ➡ **Terms to be compared** ⬇					
1.					
2.					
3.					
4.					
5.					
6.					
7.					
8.					
9.					

Personal Association Vocabulary Strategy

Directions: Use the following chart to make personal associations to a new vocabulary word.

Vocabulary Word and Illustration	Personal Association(s)
Examples	**Non-examples**

Vocabulary Explorations Through Questioning

Directions: Use the following chart to question the unusual or unknown words that you encountered in the text.

Unusual or Unknown Word: ____________________

Questions Heard	Responses
How would you use this vocabulary word in your writing or everyday conversation?	
How does this vocabulary word connect to your personal experience or prior knowledge?	
How would you teach this vocabulary word to someone else?	
Where would you expect to encounter this word in the future?	

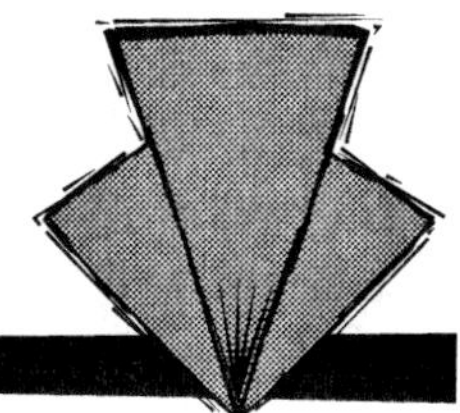

Text Coding and Vocabulary

Directions: As you read, use the codes to mark in the margins or on sticky notes next to specific vocabulary words. Then record the vocabulary word and elaborate on the code that you used to mark the text.

** = Important

? = I don't understand

?? = I wonder...

→ = This word connects to the concept because. . .

Vocabulary Word (Use the text coding to find text information.)	**Response** (Choose from the sentence starters below to get started on your response.) ** I think this word is important because. . . ? I don't understand this word because. . . ?? I wonder if this words means __________ because. . . → This word connects to the key concept because. . .

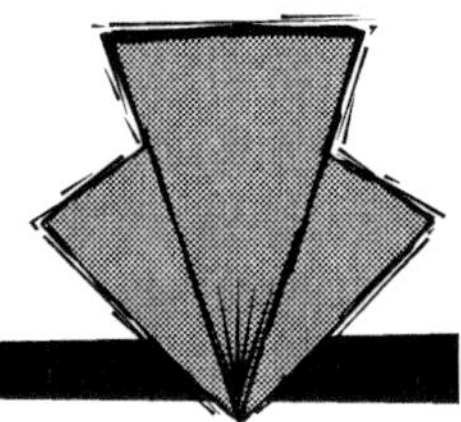

Capsule Vocabulary

Directions: Record conceptually linked vocabulary words found while speaking, listening, writing, and reading.

Capsule Vocabulary: words related to the topic

____

____

____

____

Have a conversation with your group and use as many capsule words as possible. Make a list of words used.

____

____

____

____

Listen to your teacher and record the capsule words that you hear him or her use.

____

____

____

____

Write a story and use as many capsule words as possible.

____

____

____

____

Read the text and record all of the capsule words included in the text.

____

____

____

____

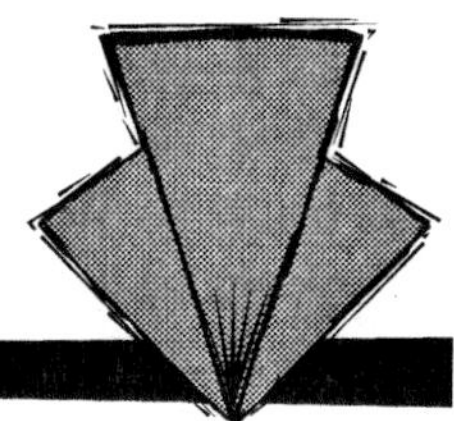

Personification Vocabulary

Vocabulary Word	Definition	Personification of Vocabulary Word

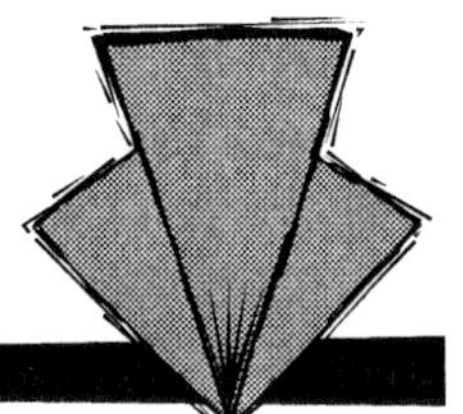

Exploring Content Vocabulary

Directions: Explore the content vocabulary connected to the topic you are studying.

Identify words that are specific to the content area that you are studying.	Choose one word. Why do you need to know this word? How will it be useful to you?
Choose a different word. How does this word connect to other words that you are learning related to this topic?	Choose yet another word. What similes or metaphors could you create using this word?
Examine all the words. Which word is the most challenging to understand? Why?	Examine all the words again. Which word is the most difficult to pronounce? Spell it phonetically in the space below.

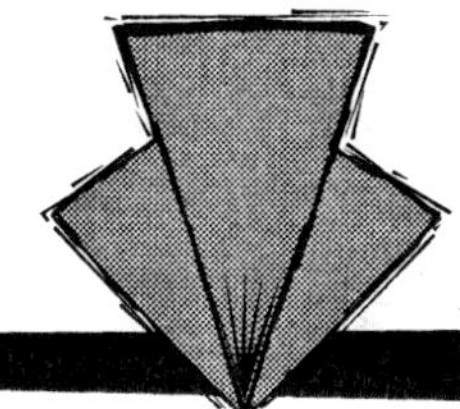

Dictionary Definitions

Directions: Use the dictionary to look up unknown vocabulary words.

Unknown Word	Guide Words at Top of Page	Pronunciation	Part of Speech	Definition

Artistic Interpretations

Directions: Identify the unknown word and use the context to write a definition. After looking up the word in a dictionary, draw a creative picture of the word. Finally, reflect on your drawing by responding to the questions at the bottom of the page.

Unknown word: ______________________________

Definition based on context: ______________________________

____

Dictionary definition: ______________________________

____

Illustration of the word: (Draw a picture that shows the word interacting with other people, places, or

What details did you add to your picture that surprised you? What are your most creative or insightful details? How could you use this word in your own life?

____

____

____

How did drawing a picture of the word help you understand the word better?

____

____

____

Prior Knowledge and Making Connections

4

Prior Knowledge and Making Connections

Introduction

Prior knowledge is everything that students have already learned. Students have prior knowledge about a topic, social experiences related to the topic, text structure, and reading strategies. Some students may have very limited prior knowledge in one or all areas; other students may have some knowledge, while still others may have quite a bit of knowledge. In the classroom, it is important to recognize the range of knowledge and experiences that students have and to provide them with a multitude of strategies that allow them to make connections between existing knowledge and new knowledge.

Connecting to Life Experiences

Secondary school students must become proficient at tapping into their deeply held cognitive structures called "schemata." Schemata (schema is singular) are the concepts that we develop about people, places, experiences, and events. For example, a small child knows the name of only one four-legged animal—"dog." Until he or she has more exposure and cognitive capacity, every four-legged animal is a dog. As the child acquires knowledge, the schema of four-legged animals expands to include cats, squirrels, and rabbits. In other words, the child assimilates or adds to the schema of four-legged animals. The child also accommodates or makes changes in previously held knowledge, that is, that there are four-legged animals other than dogs. Review with students what they already know about a topic and where they learned the information. Tapping into their life experiences is also highly motivating. After introducing a topic, here are some questions that may help students connect with their personal experiences:

- What memories do you have that connect with this topic?
- Have you ever seen a TV show about the topic?
- What feelings do you have in connection with the topic?
- Have you ever known someone who has told you about the topic? What was the person like?
- What concerns or interests you about the topic?

Asking Questions and Assessing Prior Knowledge

Questioning is a highly effective way to tap into prior knowledge. Questioning helps readers to connect new knowledge with their existing understanding. Some sample questions include:

- What do you already know about ________________________?
- When you hear the word(s) ____________________________, what do you think of?
- What events or ideas do you know that connect to the topic?

Prior Knowledge and Making Connections

Asking Questions and Assessing Prior Knowledge *(cont.)*

Other techniques also can assess prior knowledge. The following are based on suggestions from Holmes and Roser (1987):

- **Free recall:** Have students tell anything that comes to mind about a topic.
- **Word association:** Ask students what comes to mind when you provide a few keys words and phrases from the text.
- **Recognition:** Select key words and phrases associated with a text and display them along with erroneous words and phrases. Ask students which words and phrases are and are not associated with the text based upon its title.
- **Structured questions:** Preview the text and prepare a set of questions designed to assess knowledge.
- **Unstructured discussion:** Ask students what they know about a topic, such as the explorations of Lewis and Clark. (Holmes and Roser considered this method the least effective. Therefore, it is worth the preparation time required for the prior four methods.)

Evaluating Nonfiction Materials Using Prior Knowledge

Throughout their academic careers, students will need to locate and read a variety of nonfiction materials in order to access information necessary to complete their assignments. Students can use the following questions to help them evaluate nonfiction using prior knowledge.

- Is this text organized in such a way that the information makes sense?
- How will the text features help me to understand the topic?
- How does this text compare to another text on the same topic?
- What reading strategies will I need to use to make sense of the information?

Reformulating and Modifying Existing Knowledge

The purpose of learning new information is to build upon and clarify the existing information stored in a person's mind. Students must have many strategies to help them reformulate and modify their existing knowledge. Questions they can ask themselves include:

- How does this new information change what I know about the topic?
- How does this new information change what I believe about the topic?
- What new questions do I have?

Prior Knowledge and Making Connections

Adjusting and Extending a Knowledge Base

While it is important that students tap into their prior knowledge, it is also important that they understand that as they learn new information, they have the opportunity to adjust and extend their knowledge base. Often, we lead students to believe that they are simply to acquire and retain knowledge in order to pass a test or complete a unit of study. However, we must teach students that it is their responsibility to reflect on new knowledge, integrate it with their prior experiences, generate an expanded understanding of the information, and share their enriched understanding in meaningful ways. The activity on page 91 can help students to extend their understanding.

Reflecting on New Learning

Reflecting on what has been learned is essential if students are to acquire and integrate new knowledge. Students need to have the ability to ask such questions as: How does this information confirm or contradict what I already know? How can I use this information in my life? What further questions do I have?

Formulating Ideas

After students engage in a variety of activities to tap into their prior knowledge, they need to be able to connect the text to their prior knowledge both during and after reading. Remind them to generate pictures in their minds, summarize, predict, and question as they read.

Applications to Real-Life Situations

Prior knowledge and personal experiences help us to make sense of text information, but new text information feeds back into our real lives. Students need to understand that their new learning becomes the groundwork for future prior knowledge about a topic. Emphasize to students that they will need to apply what they learn in school to real-life situations and that building strong metacognitive processes will help them to make learning meaningful.

Generating an Opinion

Students must become adept at using their prior knowledge about a topic in order to generate their own opinions. By teaching students to think about what they personally believe about the topic, teachers give them a "built-in" purpose for reading whenever they encounter new text. Encourage students to challenge their beliefs about the topic, the author's beliefs, their teacher's beliefs, and their fellow classmates' beliefs.

Prior Knowledge and Making Connections

Constructing a Personal Response

When students can construct a personal response to text, they become more proficient at integrating new information. Reassure them that it is natural for them to ask such questions as they read: How does this information relate to me? How do I feel about this information? How can I use this information in my life?

Strategy 1: Text Walking and Picture Talking

Text walking (Harvey and Goudvis, 2000) is a simple strategy in which the teacher leads students through a preview of the text using the metaphor of "walking and talking." Model how to preview the text by starting at the beginning of the text and talking about each text feature as you encounter it and how it helps to understand the major topics of the text. Modeling this strategy with a book about the water cycle might sound like the following:

> ***Teacher:*** *I am going to "walk and talk" my way through this book about the water cycle. In that way I can get a sense of what this book is about and what the different text features will tell me about the topic. First, I see a heading called "Introduction." I think that I might be introduced to the concept of the water cycle and learn some general information about it. As I "walk" further through this book, I see an illustration with captions. It looks as if it is explaining the stages of the water cycle. The captions use words, such as "evaporation," "condensation," and "precipitation." I'm not sure what all those words mean, but I'm sure I will learn some new definitions when I reread the book. There are also some photographs of rain clouds that give some more information about the water cycle.*

Strategy 2: Previewing and Self-Questioning

Present students with the worksheet (page 81) that will guide them through the previewing and self-questioning process. Begin by telling them the topic they will be exploring. You may want to show them a picture, colored overhead, or video clip to build interest. Then, have students respond to the first question on the right side of the worksheet. Have them use the questions on the left side of the worksheet to preview the text in order to gather as much information as possible, using the text features for guidance. As they read, have them complete the remainder of the right side of the worksheet, making connections to their prior knowledge and thinking of ways to remember the information.

Prior Knowledge and Making Connections

Strategy 3: K-W-L and K-W-L Plus

A highly effective strategy, K-W-L structures students' thinking before and after reading. Often it is difficult to begin this activity without building some background knowledge. As a class, complete the "knowledge" portion of the K-W-L chart on page 82. Then work with students to generate questions they have about the topic and complete the center column of the chart. You may want to use this chart as a previewing activity and have students' questions result from looking at the headings, subheadings, and pictures associated with the text. Next, have students read the text. When they are finished, they record what they learned and any new questions they may have. As an extension, use the K-W-L Plus question at the bottom of the worksheet to have students reflect on the importance of the information and how they will use or apply what they have learned to their lives. Here is a completed K-W-L chart about the seasons:

What I Know	What I Want to Learn	What I Learned
There are four seasons in the year. Our weather changes with each season. Fall, winter, spring, and summer are all seasons.	What causes seasons? Do all regions have four seasons?	The changing seasons are caused by the changing position of the Earth in relation to the sun. Some regions only have two seasons, such as a wet and a dry season.

Strategy 4: Anticipation Guides

Anticipation guides are used to stimulate thinking about a topic before reading a text. An anticipation guide contains a series of statements pertaining to a topic in a piece of text students are going to read. Before reading, students determine whether the statements are true or false or whether they agree or disagree with them. As they read the assigned text, they can focus on finding information in the text that supports or disconfirms their positions. When they complete the text, they can return to the anticipation guide to see if their opinions changed or stayed the same. They can also be required to point to places in the text that caused them to maintain or change their positions.

Prior Knowledge and Making Connections

Strategy 4: Anticipation Guides *(cont.)*

Here is an example of an anticipation guide:

Topic: Abolition of Slavery

Before reading the text, read each statement and circle **A** if you agree or **D** if you disagree on the left. After you read the text, circle the statements for the way you feel on the right.

Before		**After**
A D	1. There were slaves involved in the abolition movement.	A D
A D	2. Only Northerners thought slavery should be abolished.	A D
A D	3. Before Abraham Lincoln became president, little was done to end slavery.	A D

The anticipation guide takes time to construct, but any guides that you create can be filed away for future use. The basic steps to constructing a guide are as follows:

1. Preview the text to determine the important concepts that you want students to think about.
2. Write short statements about those ideas. You need write only five to ten statements that are designed to activate prior knowledge and stimulate thinking. The statements need not be true or false statements since some of them will be based on the student's or the author's opinion.
3. Present the statements in the order in which the ideas appear in the text. (You can have students copy them into the center column of the guide, or you can type them into the column and make copies for the class.)
4. Distribute the guide. Allow time for students to complete the first part. Discuss their answers, directing them to support their positions.
5. Direct students to read the text while they evaluate their opinions. Then have them complete the second part of the guide.
6. Have a post-reading follow-up discussion concerning each statement. Have any of their opinions changed as a result of reading the text? Why?

An extended anticipation guide is a variation that requires students to write about whether the text supports their opinions. Students can either quote or paraphrase the text and refer to the page number. Permit students to disagree with an author's opinion if they can successfully create an argument that they can support with details. Anticipation guide templates are provided on pages 83 and 84.

Prior Knowledge and Making Connections

Strategy 5: Structured Previews

Some students benefit from an informal preview of text, but others need a more structured approach. Use the Structured Preview worksheet (page 85) to lead students through the text, making note of text structure, text features, key concepts/facts, predictions, and connections to prior knowledge. A structured approach will help struggling readers tap into their prior knowledge of both reading and life experiences connected to the text.

Strategy 6: Riveting Reflections

Have students tap into their prior knowledge by using the worksheet entitled Riveting Reflections (page 86). Continue by having students record what they learned after they read. Instruct them to reflect on their learning by identifying personal connections, evaluating the author, and generating questions.

Strategy 7: Predicting and Confirming Guide

Begin by having students preview the text and make predictions about the contents. Model how to create prediction statements and record them on the Predicting and Confirming Guide worksheet (page 87). Then have students read the text with the intention of finding information that either confirmed or contradicted their predictions. Students should circle "yes" or "no" in the center column of their worksheets. Finally, have them explain the information that confirmed or contradicted their predictions. They can include what surprised, confused, or disappointed them about the text information. For example, if they were previewing a text about holidays around the world, they might make predictions about the kinds of celebrations that occur on these days. They might assume that Boxing Day is related to the sport of boxing. Once they read the text, they will be able to write the new information that supported or disputed their predictions.

Strategy 8: Visual Reading Guide

The Visual Reading Guide (page 88) provides struggling readers with a framework for previewing the text features in the reading material. Have students record what they can learn from the various text features (headings, subheadings, graphs, charts, diagrams, illustrations, photographs, and captions) in the left column of the chart. Then have them connect the information that they observed with their prior knowledge. For example, in a reading selection on slavery, students may encounter a picture of Frederick Douglass. Many would record that they knew that he was an African-American writer who fought for the abolishment of slavery.

Strategy 9: Creating a Pre-Reading Plan

Judith Langer (1991) created this strategy to assess students' depth of understanding of a topic. Use the Create a Pre-Reading Plan worksheet (page 89) for students to identify words that are associated with the topic. Then have them explain how they know the words. Through discussion, students clarify and refine their connections and understandings. Also, ask them to summarize their prior knowledge and identify what they hope to learn from the reading.

Prior Knowledge and Making Connections

Strategy 10: Synthesizing Opinions

Secondary level students must have the ability to synthesize various viewpoints and generate their own opinions based on the information they have gathered. Have students complete the Synthesizing Opinions worksheet (page 90) to identify the viewpoints of the author, their teacher, another source, and another classmate. Then, instruct them to evaluate each viewpoint in order to generate their own opinion on the topic.

Strategy 11: A Scavenger Hunt

Divide students into teams and give each team an identical list of terms and concepts to find. Have the teams quickly preview the text to find the terms or concepts and develop a definition or association based on the text. The first team to finish wins.

Strategy 12: Partnered Reading

Pair each student with a partner. Discuss the topic or concept to be studied and perhaps allow them briefly to preview the text. Then have the pairs use the Partnered Reading worksheet (page 92) to identify and discuss their prior knowledge of the topic. They can compare the amount they know, the depth of their knowledge, and their interest in the topic. After reading, instruct them to identify how the text connected to their prior knowledge and determine which partner found information that most strongly connected to prior knowledge. This discussion will help them learn and retain the new information. Model the process before they begin. Below is a sample dialogue you and a student might model for the class:

Teacher: We are reading a book about geometry. I know a lot about geometry.

Student: I know a lot, too. I know that geometry is about shapes and lines.

Teacher: I can name many shapes. I'm going to write some of them on my worksheet.

Student: I've had many experiences with shapes since kindergarten, like toys that come in different shapes.

Teacher: I also know that geometry is about putting shapes together to make other shapes. I've seen that done with tangrams.

Student: I want to write the definitions of some shapes and mention how many sides and corners shapes have.

Teacher: That is good information. I will include other words associated with geometry, like parallel and angle, but I'm not sure of the definitions. Do you know the meanings?

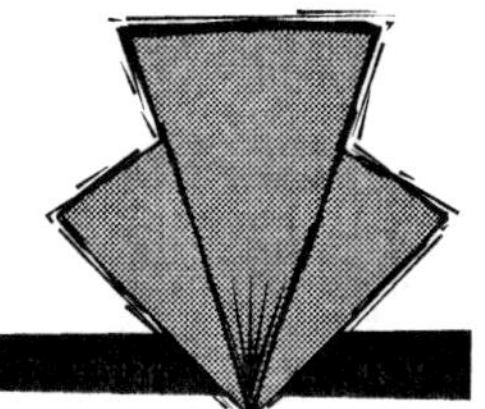

Previewing and Self-Questioning

Directions: Preview the text before reading and complete the left column. Before and during reading, answer the questions in the right column.

Previewing (Before Reading)	Self-Questioning (Before and During Reading)
What information seems to be significant and important?	What information do I already know about the topic?
Which text features seem important? (captions, charts, graphs, diagrams, maps, photographs, illustrations, headings, subheadings)	How does the information I am reading connect to what I already know? How will I remember this information?

K-W-L and K-W-L Plus

Directions: Complete the left and center columns before reading. After reading, complete the right

What do I already know?	What do I want to know?	What did I learn?
What I know: How I know:	Questions about the topic:	What I learned: What I still want to learn:

K-W-L Plus

Reflection: Why is this information important for me to know? How can I use this information?

____

____

____

____

____

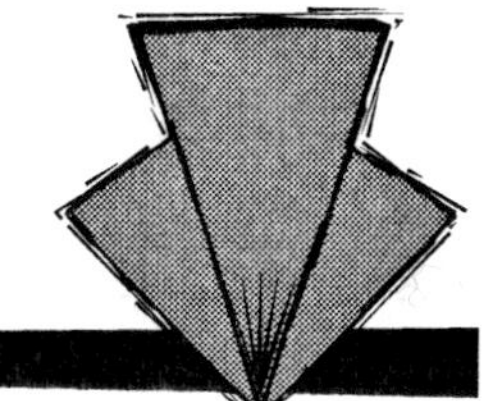

Agree or Disagree Anticipation Guide

Directions: Record statements about the topic in the center of the chart. Before reading, think about whether you agree or disagree with each statement by placing a check in the appropriate box under the "Before Reading" heading. After reading, think about the information you read and whether it changed your opinion about any of the statements about the topic. Then, place a check in the appropriate box under the "After Reading" heading.

Before Reading			***After Reading***	
Agree	**Disagree**	**Statements About the Topic**	**Agree**	**Disagree**

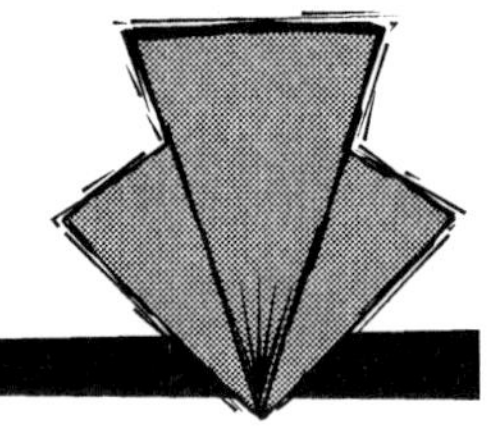

True or False Anticipation Guide

Directions: Record statements about the topic in the center of the chart. Before reading, think about whether the statements are true or false and place a check in the appropriate box under the "Before Reading" heading. After reading, think about the information you read and whether the statements are true or false. Then, place a check in the appropriate box under the "After Reading" heading.

Before Reading			*After Reading*	
True	**False**	**Statements About the Topic**	**True**	**False**

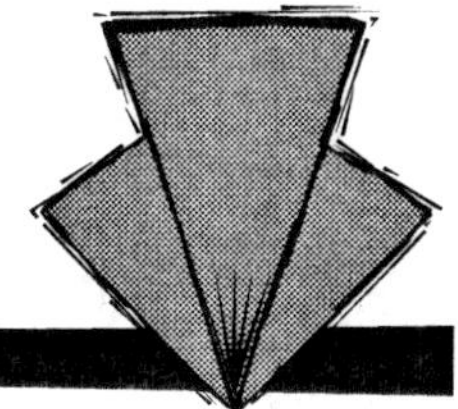

Structured Preview

Directions: Preview the text to determine these elements.

Topic: ____

Text Structure (description, compare/contrast, cause/effect, listing, problem/solution):

Text Features:

Key Concepts	Facts

Prediction about what I will learn:

How will this information connect to what I already know?

Riveting Reflections

Directions: Use the worksheet below to reflect on your new learning about the topic.

Before Reading: What do you already know about the topic? What do you expect to learn?
After Reading: What did you learn?

Personal Reaction: How did this information make you feel?	**Critical Reaction:** How could the author have done a better job?	**Questions:** What further information do you want to know?

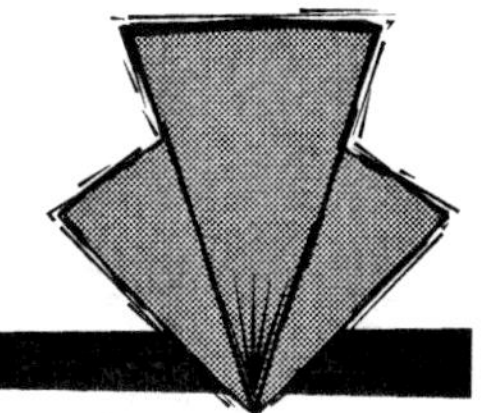

Predicting and Confirming Guide

Directions: Make predictions about what you will learn before you read. As you read, determine whether your predictions were confirmed. Then explain using text information.

Predictions About the Content (What will I learn?)	**Confirmed by the Text**	**Explanation**
	YES NO	
	YES NO	
	YES NO	
	YES NO	
	YES NO	
	YES NO	

Visual Reading Guide

Directions: Preview the text and record as many details as you can regarding the text features listed. Then identify what you already know about the information contained in these text features.

Visual Cues or Text Features	What I Already Know
Headings:	
Subheadings:	
Bolded or italicized words:	
Illustrations, photographs, and captions:	
Charts, graphs, and diagrams:	

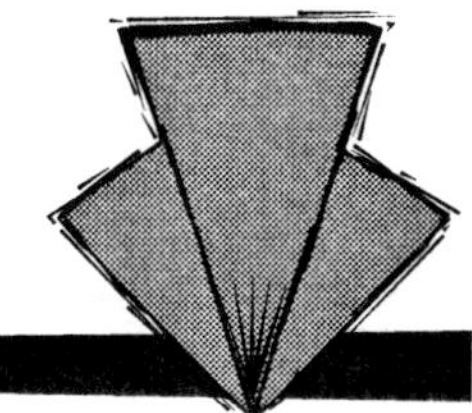

Creating a Pre-Reading Plan

Directions: Complete the following activities to make a plan for reading.

Topic: ______________________________

Make a list of words you associate with the topic:

____

____

____

Choose three words from your brainstorming above and record them in the left column of the chart below. Then answer the question in the top right column of the chart.

Words	What made you think of this word in connection with the topic?

Write a brief summary of what you already know about the topic: ______________________________

____

____

____

____

What new information do you hope to learn? ______________________________

____

____

____

____

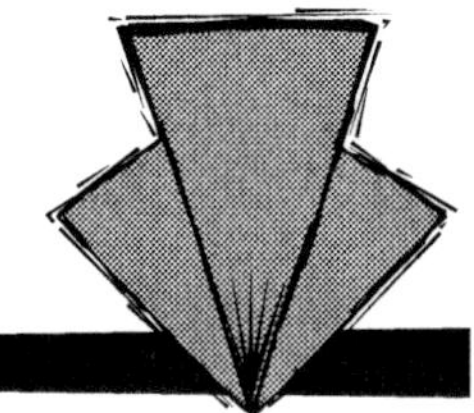

Synthesizing Opinions

Directions: Identify several different viewpoints about the topic in the article you read. Then

What does the author believe about the topic?	What does my teacher believe about the topic?
What does one other source say about the topic?	What does my classmate believe about the topic?

What do I believe about the topic?

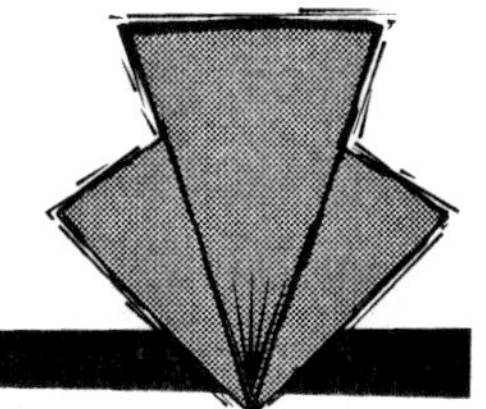

Extending What You Have Learned

Directions: Use the worksheet below to activate prior knowledge, reflect on your new learning, and extend your understanding.

Activate Your Prior Knowledge	Reflect on What You Have Learned
Before Reading: What do you already know about this topic?	After Reading: What did you learn and how does it fit with what you already know?

Create Something New to Show Your Understanding: Write a story, poem, diary entry, letter, or draw a picture.

Partnered Reading

Directions: Each partner takes turns recording prior knowledge and the connection to new knowledge. Then discuss the reflection question and record your response on the lines provided.

Topic: ______________________________

Partner 1: Prior knowledge about the topic	**Partner 2:** Prior knowledge about the topic
Partner 1: How does the information you have learned connect to your prior knowledge?	**Partner 2:** How does the information you have learned connect to your prior knowledge?

Reflection: Which partner's prior knowledge was more closely connected to the text? Explain.

____

____

____

____

Author's Point of View

Author's Point of View

Introduction

The concept of the author's viewpoint differs between fiction and nonfiction. In fiction the author creates a character, or even multiple characters, who tells the story through a created point of view. Fiction is subjective, as the characters, setting, and plot work together to evoke feelings and mood in the reader.

On the other hand, a nonfiction author's viewpoint exists on more of a continuum. A nonfiction work may be objective or subjective, neutral or biased, depending on the purpose, intended audience, and type of text. At one end of the continuum are materials that convey information, such as news articles, instruction manuals, and reference books. These materials are objective and usually written in third person. The author's personal viewpoint is omitted and is considered nonessential. At the other end of the continuum are subjective texts, such as essays, memoirs, and autobiographies in which the author's viewpoint is central to the work. Editorials are the midpoint of the continuum. Based on facts in current events, editorials contain the author's commentary on contemporary social patterns and political issues.

Of course, many texts combine both fact and opinion, either intentionally or unintentionally. For example, cookbooks are nonfiction, but cooks may differ considerably in their approaches to cooking. History books, on the other hand, are supposed to be objective; but they often contain bias. The victors in a battle, for example, may seem righteous. For anyone who pays attention to medical news, there is bias as well; witness the back-and-forth clamor over low- versus high-carbohydrate diets or the risks and benefits of Vitamin C.

Teaching students to recognize bias and to separate fact from opinion is one of the first steps in helping them recognize that nonfiction is not always "the truth." They also need to understand that fact and opinion can be found in the same piece of writing. Teaching secondary school students to develop healthy skepticism and to question the source of information is essential. The ability to form opinions and to express them requires critical thinking. Some students will be more ready than others to read critically for point of view, but this skill can be taught.

The Difference Between Fact and Opinion

When reading in the content areas, secondary school students must understand how authors use fact and opinion to achieve their purposes. Authors write nonfiction to inform, to persuade, or to entertain. When they choose their examples and supporting details in informational and persuasive writing, authors use a blend of facts and opinions.

Author's Point of View

The Difference Between Fact and Opinion *(cont.)*

Begin by presenting students with pairs of sentences, one reflecting fact and one reflecting opinion, like those shown below. Thereafter, use sentence pairs that relate to a text you currently are reading in class.

Examples

Roses need specific amounts of nitrogen, water, and sun to produce the best blooms.

All roses are most lovely when they have just the right amount of water, soil, and sun.

To be nutritious, school cafeteria menus need to include the five food groups.

When meat is included in the school cafeteria menu, it can no longer be nutritious.

Point out to students that facts are difficult to dispute. Roses do have very specific requirements; they cannot grow in the shade, for example. Opinions, on the other hand, can be debated. For example, roses may have rust and produce sparse flowers, no matter how exacting the gardener may be, so not all roses are "lovely." Discuss the second pair of sentences in the same way. The first sentence comes from well-accepted, established research; the second comes from what appears to be a vegetarian author who does not see the value of meat as part of the school menu. Opinions provoke debate; without support, they do not hold up to examination in the way that facts do. Of course, facts can be disputed as well, but usually investigation is required in order to change a fact. An opinion can be changed in an instant.

You can extend this activity by looking at paragraphs from several different sources, even seemingly objective ones, such as front page newspaper stories, and by reading them sentence by sentence to discover fact and opinion. Tell students that they will learn to think for themselves by questioning and analyzing all that they read.

To demonstrate the investigation of facts, have students write ten sentences, half of them true and half false, based on a social studies or science text that the class is currently reading. Ask them to exchange papers with a classmate. The classmate must then determine which are facts, citing page and paragraph numbers in the text. They should then correct any false sentences so that they read as facts based on the text.

Author's Point of View

Determining Point of View

Much of nonfiction writing is impersonal and, therefore, written in the third-person point of view. This point of view is the most objective, the one that best conveys facts without the intrusion of the author's thoughts, feelings, and opinions. But two other points of view—first and second—are used in different texts and for different purposes in nonfiction. For example:

- First person: Editorials, essays, autobiographies, original source material (diaries, letters, etc.), reviews, eyewitness accounts; text that conveys immediacy. Authors use first-person pronouns—I, me, my, we, us, our.
- Second person: Advertising, campaign propaganda, brochures; text with which the author wants the reader to identify. Authors use second-person pronouns—you, your, yours.
- Third person: Descriptions, chronologies, research, reports, news items, in-depth articles. Authors use third-person pronouns—he, she, they, him, her, them, his, hers, their, theirs.

Make a habit of asking students to notice the point of view whenever they begin to read a new piece of nonfiction. Ask them why the author may have chosen this point of view and how the piece would be changed if it were written from a different point of view.

Making Sense of the Author's Word Choice

The words in the text should reflect an author's knowledge of the topic with the intent of informing the reader. Informational writers use rhetorical questions, incorporate figurative language when appropriate, and vary their sentence length and structure. Most authors not only want the information to be accessible, but also want to achieve their purpose by allowing the reader to "enter" into the text comfortably by making the word choice and language interesting, compelling, and appropriate to the audience's knowledge level, age, and experiences. Also, remind students to notice the denotation and connotation of words when they examine an author's language for bias.

Using Context to Determine Author's Viewpoint

It is important for readers to understand that there is a context in which the author's viewpoint was created. Encourage students to use the following questions to determine the context: When and where did the events in the article take place? What are other events connected to the topic? What is the author's connection to the topic?

Sometimes context is irrelevant or difficult to determine. When working with many different kinds of text, it may be challenging to get information about the author and his or her connection to the topic. However, when appropriate, provide students with information about the author and his or her connection to the topic and any other outside information relevant to the topic that might help to determine any bias.

Author's Point of View

Evaluating the Author's Viewpoint

Some strategies presented in this section are intended to guide you in helping students recognize and evaluate the author's point of view. The following questions may help students evaluate the author's effectiveness: Did the author use an appropriate balance of facts and opinions? Is the author's bias toward the topic apparent? What information should the author have added? What information could the author delete? What questions do you have for the author?

Strategy 1: Question/Answer Role-playing

Assign students the role of the reader while you assume the role of the author. After students read a text together, have them engage in a spontaneous question/answer period. A reader will ask the "author" about his or her choices of organizational structure, word selection, examples, and language. The author will ask the readers' questions pertaining to clarity of ideas and language. The author may also ask what the readers want to know more about. This process may be difficult at first because students will have to become familiar with using the inferencing skills necessary to complete this activity. Model a dialogue in which you assume the role of author and a student assumes the role of the reader. The following example could occur after reading a text on Helen Keller:

Student/Reader: I thought your biography of Helen Keller was informative and interesting. How did you choose the organization of your writing?

Teacher/Author: I figured that readers would want to know about her life from start to finish, so I wrote the story chronologically from her birth to her death.

Student/Reader: You spent a lot of time writing about Annie Sullivan. That made me realize how important she was to Helen Keller.

Teacher/Author: I wanted to convey that exact idea. Annie Sullivan was responsible for teaching Helen to communicate with the world. She really changed her entire life.

Student/Reader: When you said that Helen was determined to see and hear in any way possible, what did you mean? I thought she was blind and deaf and could not see or hear.

Teacher/Author: I wrote that because she really learned to see and hear things in her own way. She might not have been able to do those things the way we can, but she learned other ways of communicating that made it possible for her to understand the world around her.

Student/Reader: The pictures of her traveling around the world and sharing her story made me understand how brave she really was.

Teacher/Author: I thought it was important to show real pictures of her. People tend to forget she was a real person because they hear so many things about her life.

Author's Point of View

Strategy 2: Fact vs. Opinion

Have students read text that contains a blend of facts and opinions. Pair them with partners to generate a quiz that contains only questions about the facts in the text. Have them switch papers with another pair and answer the fact-based questions. Then give them a chart with three categories: facts, the author's opinion of the topic, my opinion of the topic. Have them complete the chart and then discuss with them the differences between fact and opinion, as well as the similarities and differences between their opinions and the author's opinions. As a variation, have students work with a partner and use a chart (page 104) to record facts from the text and the opinions of each partner. Make sure to emphasize that authors use a blend of facts and opinions intentionally to achieve their purpose. Also, have them practice separating fact from opinion by completing the worksheet on page 105.

Strategy 3: Point of View

Students may need practice in recognizing first-, second-, and third-person point of view. The worksheet on page 106 gives them more information about the three points of view and gives them practice in rewriting and changing a point of view and writing from one point of view.

Strategy 4: Biased and Non-biased Storytelling

With students sitting in a large circle, tell two simple stories about your morning. The first story should include language that is calm, reasonable, and non-biased. Present only the facts. The second story should involve the same information but should include overly emotional, biased judgments about the morning's events. Then give students a topic, such as "our school hallways" or "summertime." Going around the circle, have each tell one non-biased sentence about the topic. Then go around again with each telling one sentence that is overly emotional and judgmental. Discuss the importance of using reasonable, rational language and examples when presenting information in order to prove their credibility as writers. The following example of a factual story might be helpful:

> *This morning I woke up to the sound of my alarm clock. I fed my cat and made breakfast for my family. Then I showered. I got dressed and brushed my teeth. I said goodbye to my family and got in my car. It was raining, so I drove carefully. I got to school and came to the classroom to get ready for the day.*

The same story told with opinionated language might sound like the following:

> *Waking to the annoying sound of my alarm clock was the worst way to start my day. I had to feed my meowing cat right away or he would follow me around all morning. I started to make breakfast for my family, but I was rushing and accidentally burned the toast. I rushed out the door and almost forgot my keys. It was raining, and I was so upset because I hate the rain. Every other car was driving like crazy. I arrived at school and rushed to class before the bell rang. It was a hectic morning.*

Author's Point of View

Strategy 5: Biased Viewpoints in the News

Students need to be able to separate objective reporting from biased writing. Biased writing occurs when the author or the publication has a particular slant or prejudice that affects the way in which news is reported. A conservative newspaper and a liberal newspaper will report about the same event in very different ways. To determine bias in a piece of writing, students must be able to make inferences from the language of the author. They must be able to get beneath the literal meaning, the surface meaning, of the author's words to determine the author's deeper meaning and influence.

Use the activity on page 107 to initiate a discussion on bias with students. In the meantime, collect a variety of brief newspaper articles from a few different newspapers. Ask around; you may find people who get out-of-town newspapers as well. If possible, try to find articles about the same topic. Use them with your students and conduct exercises similar to the one found on page 108.

Strategy 6: Writing with Bias

Students can also learn about bias by writing their own articles. Give students a set of facts such as the following:

- A developer wants to build houses on a bluff overlooking the ocean.
- The city council wants to limit the number of houses being built.
- The bluff currently is used for recreation by hikers and mountain bikers.

Have students pick the persona of one of the following reporters:

- A reporter for a local weekly newspaper that serves only people living around the bluff.
- A reporter for a big daily newspaper that supports local business.
- A reporter for a small daily newspaper that is pro-environment.

Allow time for sharing and discussing their reports. Have students listen for and identify evidence of bias in each other's work. Use the Objectivity in the News worksheet on page 109.

Author's Point of View

Strategy 7: Persuasive Points of View: Editorials

Opinion and bias, both intentional and unintentional, are two means by which authors express their points of view. Sometimes, however, authors have a straightforward task, which is to persuade the reader to adopt the same viewpoint as their own. Authors give the reader good reasons to change his or her mind about a subject or event. Editorials accomplish this task. A well-written editorial gives the opinion of the author and also attempts to persuade the reader of his or her point of view. Expose students to a variety of editorials. Point out their relationship to current events, the author's opinion, and the persuasive language that the author uses to sway the reader. You may use the exercise on page 110 to initiate your discussion.

Strategy 8: Compare and Contrast

Collect news articles and editorials on the same subject matter or event. Have students compare and contrast the author's viewpoint, e.g., subjective vs. objective, neutral vs. biased, etc. Also have them jot down the factual information found in each type of writing. Discuss the language that the authors used. Ask students about the emotional content of each type of writing. Which used more adverbs and adjectives? Did one piece use metaphors or other imagery to make a point to the reader? Is there evidence of bias in the supposedly neutral article?

You may have students use a Venn diagram to help them organize their thinking. Either as a class or individually, have them list facts included in both types of writing within the intersection and the other content in the remaining parts of the circles.

Strategy 9: Letters to the Editor

Letters to the editor are a vital part of any newspaper. In such letters readers can point out what they believe to be an author's bias, make an argument against an editorial writer, or make a point that an author may have missed. Pick a controversial newspaper editorial or article for students to read; then follow the letters to the editor that respond to it. Study the editorial and rebuttal letters to determine the author's point of view. How does each writer use the facts to support his or her argument? What emotional language does each writer use to sway the reader? As an extension, encourage students to write their own letters to the editor, either individually or as a class.

Author's Point of View

Strategy 10: Propaganda Techniques

Secondary school students have been exposed to thousands of commercials and advertisements through television, radio, magazines, and even the Internet. Teaching them to recognize the different techniques used by the media and advertisers to get the public to buy their products and services will help them to become critical readers.

Begin by explaining the eight common propaganda techniques:

Testimonial—Persuasive statements made by people (often celebrities or sport's stars) who claim to have personal experience with the product. For example, the basketball star selling soap claims it cleans better than other soaps, even though he is not an expert on soap.

Bandwagon—These statements want to make the reader believe that everyone is buying the product. For example, "Everyone loves our new breakfast cereal. Try Granny's Branies."

Name-calling—These statements claim that one product is better than another. They represent other products, services, or ideas negatively. "Cleano is not gritty like Ajax."

Facts Left Out—Statements leave out facts that may influence the reader not to buy the product. For example, cigarette ads that have the Surgeon General's warning about the dangers of smoking in very small print at the bottom of the ad.

Opinions as Facts—These statements present opinions as factual information. "This watch is the most accurate timekeeper. It is the most attractive one I've seen."

Use of Numbers and Statistics—The author uses statistics to give the subject greater importance. "Nine out of 10 hospitals give this pain medicine to their patients."

Quotation out of Context—The writer quotes a source without giving the entire quotation. "This book should be on everyone's list. . . ." Left out was the rest of the quote "to keep out of the hands of children because it has too much violence and racist characters."

Red Herring—These statements are intended to mislead the reader. "Wash-O laundry detergent makes your clothes smell fresh and clean." This ad doesn't say it cleans the clothes.

Students can bring in examples of each technique, or use appropriate magazines and newspapers you have collected to provide them with materials to use in the classroom. Students can work in pairs or groups to create a poster with one example of each technique or a poster collage with many examples of one specific propaganda technique. Groups or partners can explain their posters to the class, or they can read examples from their posters and have the class identify which technique the poster illustrates. Display the posters around the classroom. The Avoiding Bias worksheet on page 112 gives students practice in identifying each propaganda technique.

Author's Point of View

Strategy 11: Personal Points of View—Essays, Memoirs, and Autobiographies

Essays, memoirs, and autobiographies represent a special form of nonfiction. A single truth—the author's—forms the basis for these types of writings. For this reason, generally they are the strongest expression of a nonfiction writer's point of view. These writings contain more voice, reflecting the writer's personal expression through choice of language and attention to detail. Though more personal, essays, memoirs, and autobiographies may still carry a theme or persuade the reader to a particular point of view. Use the following examples to discuss with students the points of view or voice that can be found in this type of writing.

ironic	sarcastic	mournful
shameless	heroic	stodgy
dramatic	self-pitying	adamant
funny	angry	

You can see that it can be quite challenging to come up with just the right adjectives to describe an author's point of view. Gather examples of essays and such to share with students. Have them discuss the "truth" of what the author is stating. Discuss the fictional devices that the nonfiction writer might employ in order to strengthen his or her voice, e.g., metaphor, irony, and personification. See pages 113 and 114 for practice.

Fact/Opinion Partner Chart

Directions: With your partner read the assigned text to find as many facts as you can on your topic. Write facts from the text in the left column. Each partner writes an opinion in his or her column for each fact.

Facts from Text	Opinions of Partner 1	Opinions of Partner 2

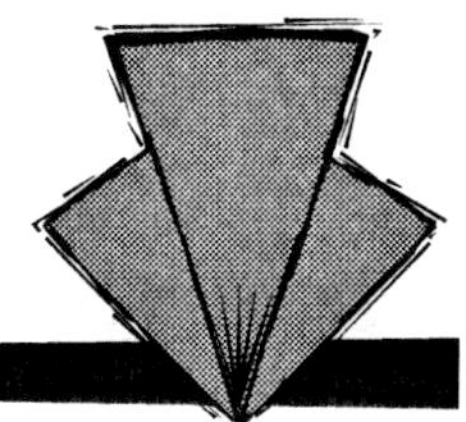

Separating Fact from Opinion

Directions: Many types of nonfiction contain opinions as well as facts. Opinions are statements that can be debated because they are based on information that cannot be proven. Facts are statements that can be proved and are not easily argued. To change a factual statement, there may even need to be experimentation or investigation. Read the statements below and determine which is an opinion and which is a fact.

Peppermint makes a refreshing ice tea.

Peppermint can be used to help settle an upset stomach.

The first statement contains an opinion. The statement can be debated because people who dislike peppermint would not find a tea made from it refreshing. The second statement is a fact. Mint has been used in many cultures to help ease the stomach. Also, the second statement uses conditional language. It says that peppermint can be used; it does not say peppermint must be used.

Often, opinions make generalizations, while facts are very specific. Read the statements below and determine which is broad and which is specific.

For many young people, listening to loud music helps them release tension.

Everyone loves to relax by dancing and listening to music.

The second statement, an opinion, is broad. Look at the language of the sentence. The word *everyone* means just that. Is this statement true? Does everyone love to relax by listening to music? The first statement, a fact, is specific. It contains specific adjectives—many, young, loud. If you investigated the statement, you would most likely find that it is true, or very nearly so.

Directions: Read the statements below. Place an **O** on the lines of the ones that are opinions and an **F** on the lines for facts.

______ 1. No one likes to go to the beach when it is cold.

______ 2. Many people save money at the market by clipping coupons.

______ 3. Cats are always annoying.

______ 4. Green is a restful color for a bedroom.

______ 5. Hummingbirds move very quickly as they travel from flower to flower.

______ 6. The best way to cook a potato is by boiling.

______ 7. To keep gardens free of weeds, use plenty of mulch such as wood chips.

______ 8. All toddlers love to chew on plain bagels.

______ 9. Many people give one another flowers on Valentine's Day.

______ 10. The best cake for a party is chocolate.

First-, Second-, and Third-Person Point of View

Like fiction, nonfiction can be written from three different points of view. Which one is used will depend on the type of writing and the author's purpose.

First-person point of view

- "I" is the narrator
- Subjective writing that includes opinions and feelings
- Eyewitness accounts, editorials, autobiographies, essays, reviews
- Example: I will remember the Northridge earthquake.

Second-person point of view

- Refers to "you" in the narrative
- Writing that the author wants the reader to identify with
- Advertising, propaganda, campaign messages
- Example: Your vote is needed to put a stop to ocean pollution.

Third-person point of view

- Objective writing that omits opinions and feelings
- News items, in-depth articles, reports, research, history and science texts, how-to manuals
- Example: To assemble, insert Tab A in Slot B and give one-quarter turn.

Directions: Complete the following activities:

1. Rewrite the following in the third person point of view, as if you were writing a subjective report. Share your paragraph with classmates.

   As the flood waters rose, I began to grab belongings and hauling them out to the car. I heard a tree branch snap in the wind, then fall to the ground with a thunderous crunch. My neighbor's windshield was demolished! I jumped into my own car and sped away. Water completely covered the bridge. I turned around, knowing my only hope was to go further inland where hopefully the rain hadn't fallen so hard.

2. Find a paragraph in a news item and rewrite it in the first-person point of view. Be creative and add interesting details such as your own thoughts and feelings. Share your paragraph with classmates.
3. Write an advertisement for a popular soft drink in the second-person point of view. Try to get your reader motivated to buy the product by identifying with what you write. Share your ad with your

Newspaper Reporting: Objective and Biased

Reporters who write objectively give the reader facts, rather than opinions. However, most newspapers have a bias, or viewpoint, that may cause news to be reported in a way that goes beyond fact. Unless you know about the bias of a newspaper, you may not understand that the newspaper writer is trying to change the way you think about events.

Directions: Read the articles and the annotations (notes) below and think about the bias of the author.

Article 1

The consumer won yet another battle against big tobacco companies. Yesterday, Tom Smith of Wheezeburg, Virginia, won a lawsuit against the Green Leaf Tobacco Co., for whom Mr. Smith worked for many years. Smith claimed that the Green Leaf Tobacco Co., poisoned its workers by giving them free cigarettes. Smith suffers from lung cancer and he has not been able to quit his smoking habit. He blames his smoking habit on his employer. A spokesman for the Green Leaf Tobacco Co., says that they will appeal the decision.

Article 2

The Green Leaf Tobacco Co., will appeal the lawsuit won yesterday by bitter ex-worker Tom Smith. Smith claimed that the free cigarettes given to him by Green Leaf Tobacco Co., caused his lung cancer. However, spokespeople for Green Leaf said that Smith did not have to take the free cigarettes. In fact, Smith continued to smoke even after he knew he had cancer. Smith appeared smug over the judge's decision, stating, "I knew justice would prevail."

- Notice the first sentence of each report tells you about the author's viewpoint. One article seems to cheer for Mr. Smith; the other for the tobacco company.
- Both articles objectively report that the tobacco company gave free cigarettes to Mr. Smith.
- While both articles tell that Mr. Smith has lung cancer, one article infers (suggests) that Mr. Smith got cancer because the company gave him cigarettes. The other article infers that Mr. Smith caused his own cancer by accepting the cigarettes from the company.
- The articles end in different ways, too. The first article objectively reports that the tobacco company will appeal the decision, while the second makes a judgmental statement that Mr. Smith appeared smug, or pleased enough to be annoying to other people (especially, one might think, the reporter).

Clearly, one newspaper supports big business, while the other supports the consumer, the common person on the street. Each newspaper is trying to influence the reader in some way. When you read a newspaper, you need to be aware of its bias so that you can figure out the facts and then think of your own opinion.

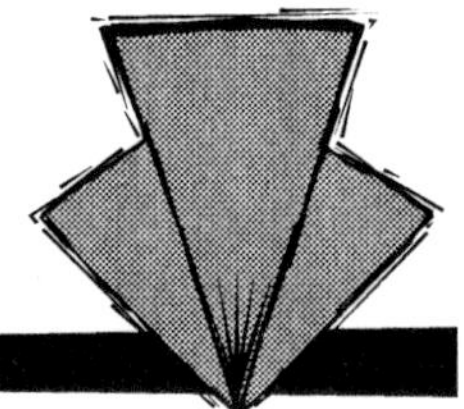

Newspaper Reporting: Objective and Biased *(cont.)*

Directions: Reread the articles on page 149 and complete the following activities:

1. Write down the facts as you understand them on the lines below.

   a. ______________________________

   b. ______________________________

   c. ______________________________

   d. ______________________________

   e. ______________________________

2. Now write your opinion about the facts. Which side do you support? Why?

   ____

   ____

   ____

   ____

3. What headline or title do you think each author would write for his or her article? Write your idea for each headline on the lines below.

   ____

   ____

   ____

   ____

4. Rewrite the article so that it is objective (that is, so that it tells only the facts) on the lines below.

   ____

   ____

   ____

   ____

Extension: Read a newspaper article on your own. Write down the facts that you gather from the article. Then write your own opinion based on the facts. Is your opinion different from the author's?

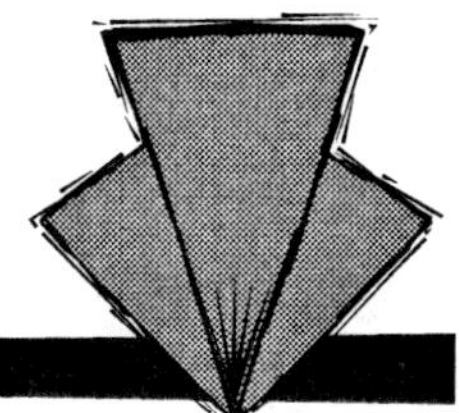

Objectivity in the News

Directions: In general, news reports are supposed to be objective, omitting feelings and opinions. Instead, news reporters rely on observations and quotes from people who participated in or witnessed the news event. Read the following news sentences and write an **O** next to the ones that are objective, and an **S** next to the ones that are subjective, or that contain emotional language.

________ 1. Bombs exploded over the desert today when Northern planes flew over the small island.

________ 2. It was a terrible sight to see resident Tony Fick crying as he looked at the damage to his seaside home.

________ 3. Temperatures are cooler than expected for this time of year due to an offshore pattern.

________ 4. The courtroom audience held its breath as the judge read the guilty verdict to the court.

________ 5. Once quiet Crystal Creek will be disturbed today as bulldozers rumble through, clearing trees and brush for a new road.

________ 6. Investigators are still trying to determine if the bees that stung two workers on Thursday were Africanized or domestic.

________ 7. Teacher Alison Freehorn of Zenith School District was nominated as this year's teacher of the year.

________ 8. There is nothing sadder than the aftermath of an automobile accident.

________ 9. The construction of a much-needed soccer field was delayed once more as city council members wrestle each other over the question of budget.

________ 10. The giant theater company, struck by hard times, is closing twenty of its megaplex theaters.

Extension: Find 3–5 newspaper articles and copy the lead sentences for each. Comment on whether the sentences are objective or not. Support your opinion by pointing out language use.

Persuasive Points of View: Editorials

When an author's purpose is to change your mind, he or she uses persuasion. Persuasion means to influence someone by providing support for his or her viewpoint. Persuasion is not the same as opinion. When an author expresses an opinion, the purpose is not necessarily to persuade the reader, but simply share a belief. A piece of persuasive writing, however, may be based on the author's opinion. Editorials are a type of persuasive writing found in newspapers. These are persuasive pieces of writing about current events, such as upcoming elections.

Directions: Read the annotated editorial below to see how the author used persuasion to influence the reader's thinking.

Western County does not need a new toll road. Two major freeways and three highways already serve its citizens. These roads are crowded at times, but even the Commissioner's own panel admits that only those drivers who can afford it will use the toll road. Therefore, the toll road will only slightly improve traffic for the rest of us, who will still be toughing it out on older roads that run through the less scenic parts of the city. For, as you know, the toll road will plow through pristine canyons. Sure, the designers have thought to put in tunnels beneath the road so that wildlife can pass from one side of the road to the other without risk of harm. I ask you, however, when was the last time you saw a deer hoofing it through a cement underpass? The luxury sedan drivers of our county should not benefit at the risk of losing our most beautiful resource—our beautiful canyons, our varied wildlife.

- The author begins with a straightforward opinion.
- The author gives support to the opinion with facts: mainly drivers who can afford tolls will drive on the toll road, and the toll road will affect wildlife.
- The word "plow" gives a visual image of the toll road as an aggressor on the canyons.
- The author asks the reader to question the toll road design by providing a difficult-to-imagine scene.
- The author makes an observation about social class by suggesting that the county's wildlife belongs to everyone and should not be used to help the wealthy get to where they need to go faster.

Extension: Find a controversial article in the newspaper about which you have a strong opinion. Think about the most important facts in the article and use them in an argument that will persuade the reader to think as you think. Share your editorial with your classmates.

Evaluating the Author s Word Choice

Part I Directions: Read the examples of text below and identify whether the examples are specific and controlled or biased and overly emotional. Use a plus sign to identify precise, controlled language and a minus sign to identify biased, highly emotional language.

1. During the Civil War, the North and the South fought valiantly, but in the end the North triumphed and the slaves were freed.

   Plus (+) or minus (–) sign: ____________________

2. The Civil War was stupid! I agree that slavery was wrong, but there must have been a smarter way to end slavery. I think it is tragic that so many lives were lost because the opposing sides were too pigheaded to figure out a solution.

   Plus (+) or minus (–) sign: ____________________

Part II Directions: Reread the text and record specific sentences that illustrate the author's word choice in the left column. Then use a plus sign to indicate precise word choice or a minus sign to indicate biased or overly emotional word choice in the right column.

Examples from the Text of the Author's Word Choice	Evaluation of the Author's Word Choice

Avoiding Bias

Directions: Read the propaganda techniques listed in Part I. Label each of the sentences in Part II with the correct propaganda technique.

Testimonial—persuasive statements made by people who claim to have personal experience with the issue

Bandwagon—statements intended to make the reader believe that "everyone is doing or believing" what the author is writing about

Name-calling—represents any alternative viewpoints negatively

Facts Left Out—leaves out facts that may influence the reader toward the author's viewpoint

Opinions as Facts—represents the opinions of the author as factual information

Use of Numbers and Statistics—gives the subject greater importance

Quotation Out of Context—quotes the source of information without providing all the information

Red Herring—information intended to mislead the reader

Part II

Sentence or Scenario	Propaganda Technique
"My teammates are a bunch of idiots. They always yell insults at the other team. They are obnoxious bullies!"	
"Eighty-seven percent of veterinarians say that this dog food is the most nutritious for dogs. Ninety-nine percent of dog owners agree."	
"The bracelet is the most beautiful one I've ever seen. It is exquisite and dazzling."	
"Everyone agrees that our vaporizer is the best for helping kids recover from colds. Moms everywhere are buying this vaporizer. Please join moms from around the country and purchase our vaporizer."	
"This exercise equipment results in bigger, stronger muscles." (The advertisement left out the fact that the equipment causes many back injuries.)	
"The characters in the movie are one of a kind." The following information was omitted from the quotation: "They were rude, fake, and unbelievable!"	
"I can attest to the quality of this vacuum cleaner. I have used it for the past thirty years and LOVE it!"	
"This dish detergent will leave your hands soft and smooth." (This ad misled the reader because it failed to mention whether the detergent actually cleans dishes!)	

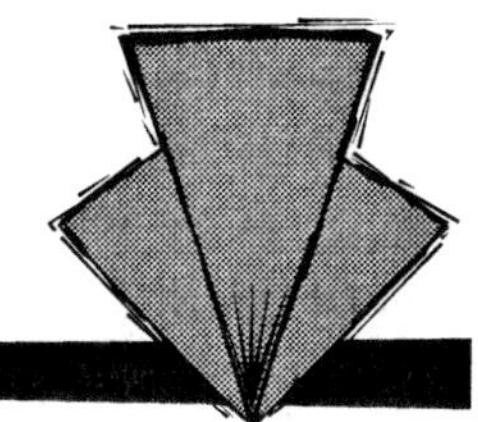

Evaluating Author s Voice

Directions: Use the following graphic organizer to analyze the author's voice.

Remember: Voice is the way the author talks about a subject that reveals his or her personality as well as beliefs or feelings about the subject. Words that describe author's voice in text include: excited, enthusiastic, cynical, skeptical, judgmental, angry, concerned, frustrated, positive, and negative.

Topic: ____________________________________

Intended Audience: ______________________________

Author's Purpose: ______________________________

____

Words to Describe the Author's Voice	Support from Text

Author's Point of View

The Essay

Essays are very personal nonfiction writings. Essays can be about something unusual that happened to the author, or they can be about an everyday occurrence that the author sees in an unusual way. The personal tone of an essay invites the reader to get to know the author and to share in understanding. Essays are read for pleasure rather than information.

Directions: Read the following essay and complete the activities below.

> *Simple pleasures are slowly disappearing from American life. Taking a stroll down a shady lane, feeding ducks a package of day-old bread, and looking for animals in the clouds have been replaced by television, movies, and video and computer games. Ask any child whether he or she would rather roll down a muddy hill or guide a hiccuping pink dinosaur on a skateboard through a maze and you know what the answer will be. The video game will win out, and the chance for a little getting-to-know-you conversation will be lost.*
>
> *Decades ago, a movie was a treat, as was a chance to play a game of pinball. Nowadays, easy entertainment is everywhere. Why make an effort when, at the click of the button, a child can escape into a world more colorful than most adults can provide? It may come as no surprise, then, that I recently had to beg my daughter to join me on a walk in a sunny canyon overlooking the ocean. At first she dragged her feet, sad to be torn away from yet another movie about a loser team coming out as winners. But soon little lizards shot around this way and that, and rabbits, too. A coyote stumbled up onto the path. A hawk wheeled overhead. Wild flowers bloomed everywhere.*
>
> *Soon we were talking about life, the universe, and everything. And at the end of the walk, my daughter said, "You know what, Mom? That was really fun." Telling her friends about an encounter with a real coyote beat watching a cartoon about one any day. A simple pleasure, to be sure, but unlike the hiccuping dinosaur, the coyote, with its black-tipped ears and delicate snout, would never be forgotten.*

Activities

1. What is the author's point of view in this essay? (First person, second person, etc.) Why is it written in this point of view?
2. With what parts of the essay, if any, do you identify as a reader?
3. What is the message, or the author's "truth," contained in the essay?

Extension: Write your own essay about something you used to do regularly that you don't do any more. Think about the tone of your essay. Are you happy or unhappy that the task or ritual is in the past? How can you let the reader know how you feel?

Structural Patterns

Structural Patterns

Introduction

Authors organize and present information using different structures in order to affect the reader in different ways. Well-written text will reflect unity and coherence because the ideas will be organized and the relationships between and among ideas will be made clear to the reader. However, students often encounter "inconsiderate" text in which the ideas are not presented clearly and the relationships between or among ideas are vague, disorganized, or non-existent. If students understand how structural patterns are used, they will be able to make sense of well-written text easily. In addition, if students encounter "inconsiderate" text, they will know why the information seems inaccessible and analyze the text by using their knowledge of structural patterns.

Authors of nonfiction texts utilize many different structures, all unified by the fact that they are organized around topics and their details. There are five generally recognized structures or patterns in content textbooks:

1. **chronological order** (also known as logical, sequential, or order and sequence)
2. **compare and contrast**
3. **cause and effect**
4. **proposition and support** (also known as problem and solution)
5. **progression of ideas** (also known as description and listing or description and collection)

The authors of nonfiction use these patterns to arrange and connect ideas. Most writers typically employ several structural patterns in the same text. Only occasionally is the entire book organized around just one pattern.

Chronological, Logical, and Sequential Order

When authors want to show a sequence of events, ideas, or steps, they will use narrative, chronological, or sequential order as a text structure. Often, chronological text in social studies will tell the story of a battle, the life of a historical figure, or the forming of a new nation. Sequential text in science will outline the steps of an experiment. In math, sequential text will describe the steps of a particular problem-solving process. Make sure to model how to identify sequential order and how to apply this structural approach to their own writing. Signal words that indicate chronological text include: "next," "first," "last," "second," "another," "then," "before," "additionally," "earlier," "later," and "finally."

Structural Patterns

Compare and Contrast

Often authors will want to show the similarities and differences between or among various topics or ideas and therefore will use a compare-and-contrast structural pattern. For example, a social studies text may delineate the similarities and differences between the Native Americans and the European colonists or among fascist, democratic, socialist, and communist forms of government. A science text may compare various chemical reactions or various geological time periods. A math text may compare different ways to solve a particular kind of problem. Compare and contrast may involve an element of analysis because the writer may include an evaluation of which method, approach, or idea is better. Astute readers need to be aware of how their feelings about the topic are being shaped. Signal words for compare and contrast include: "however," "while," "but," "rather," "most," "unlike," "like," "by contrast," "yet," "in comparison," "although," "whereas," "similar to," "similarly," "opposites," "different from," "as well as," "likewise," "on the other hand," "conversely," and "instead."

Cause and Effect

When authors want to show the relationship between events and consequences, they will often choose a cause-and-effect structure. Often there is a discernable if/then pattern that the reader will be able to recognize. It is important to teach students that even though causes have related effects, there is often a slightly more complicated element to this structure in which the effects are often the "cause" of a new problem which has a new "effect." Cause-and-effect structures show readers the relationship between ideas and events. Critical readers should be taught how to determine when a writer is making illogical leaps and attempting to assign a cause-and-effect relationship without adequate support. Signal words for cause and effect include: "consequently," "because," "since," "nevertheless," "due to," "this led to," "then. . . so," "for this reason," "on account of," "thus," "so that," "if. . . then," "therefore," "as a result," "thereby," "leads to," and "consequently."

Structural Patterns

Proposition and Support

When texts are arranged in a proposition-and-support structure, the writer proposes a proposition, hypothesis, theory, or problem and offers examples to support the theory or solve the problem. For example, the writer may propose a neighborhood cleanup. Support for this idea may include: 1. A neighborhood cleanup will get the community involved and interacting with each other in a positive way. 2. More people working together will help get the job done quickly. 3. If one community cleans up its neighborhood, maybe other communities will follow suit. Setting a good example will ultimately make a cleaner earth.

The proposition-and-support structure is great for persuasive pieces of writing including editorials. Writers may include the pros and cons for the solution. This approach relies heavily on persuasive techniques because the writer often has a particular solution in mind and will craft the text to prove his or her solution. Critical readers need to be taught how to recognize bias and how to evaluate whether or not an argument is balanced. Signal words include those used for cause and effect, as well as "propose," "conclude," "research shows," "the evidence is," "a reason for," "a solution," "the problem" or "the question."

Progression of Ideas

When writers use a progression-of-ideas structure, they list key features about the topic and elaborate on each one. For example, a social studies text may list various features of a geographic region, such as India or Saudi Arabia. These features may include government, religion, currency, economy, language, etc. A science text may list various characteristics of a particular species. Readers need to become aware of the pattern of a progression-of-ideas format: feature, details; feature, details; feature, details. Often this pattern is offset by headings and subheadings. Progression of ideas is intended to teach the reader about the topic. Critical readers then need to piece together the relationship among ideas.

Recognizing Structural Patterns

Model how to determine text structure, author's purpose, and reasons for using specific structures. Because authors often use a combination of two or more structures, it is not always clear which structure the author chose. Share your confusions and questions so students recognize how challenging the identification of text structure can be. Emphasize that learning about text structure helps to understand text and to know how to use various structures in one's own writing. Students can identify text structures in small groups and eventually on their own. Allow them to apply this knowledge to their own writing since application will build their independence with analyzing and using different structures.

Structural Patterns

Strategy 1: Description Tree

Use the Description Tree on page 123 to have students brainstorm details related to one topic. For example, if students are going to brainstorm about their summer vacations, they would write "summer vacation" in the empty box at the top of the organizer. Then, they would select two aspects of summer vacation, such as soccer camp and a trip to the beach. As they proceed in completing the graphic organizer, they would continue to generate details that are more and more specific. Finally, they would use the ideas from their graphic organizers to write paragraphs or essays about their summer vacations. You can also use this organizer to have students identify details in a text written in a progression-of-ideas pattern.

Strategy 2: Captivating Calendar Pages

Collect calendar pages with pictures of places, people, and things. Once you have several calendar pages, conduct the following compare-and-contrast activity. Divide students into groups of four. Give each group two calendar pages and Compare/Contrast Organizer I (page 124) and have them work together to identify the similarities and differences. Then, give each group three different calendar pages and complete Compare/Contrast Organizer II (page 125). Have students share their organizers. Then, introduce students to a compare-and-contrast text and have them apply their skills to the text. This strategy can be used to compare a variety of subjects, such as comparing and contrasting authors, historical events, geographical regions, or animal species. Another type of graphic organizer that works well with comparing and contrasting is the Venn diagram (page 126).

Strategy 3: Comparison Matrix

Use the organizer on page 127 to have students identify as many features of fruit as they can (sweet, nutritious, grows on trees, juicy, textured, etc.) in the left column. Then, show students several different kinds of fruit and record these kinds in the top part of the chart. Discuss with students each piece of fruit and its corresponding features, placing a check in the appropriate boxes if the fruit exemplifies a particular feature. Make the connection to text by reading information that identifies the features of a particular topic, comparing similar topics against the list of features. For example, students can identify the features of the American Revolutionary War and then compare this war directly to the War of 1812, the Civil War, WWI, and WWII by using the comparison matrix technique.

Strategy 4: Cause-Effect Morning Memories

Have students recall events from their mornings, such as the ride to school or eating breakfast, and use the Cause-and-Effect Organizer (page 128) to identify the cause-effect relationships connected with their morning memories. Be sure to have them read a cause-and-effect text and apply their knowledge of these relationships to their reading. The examples on page 122 show how students understand cause and effect in their own lives.

Strategy 4: Cause-Effect Morning Memories (cont.)

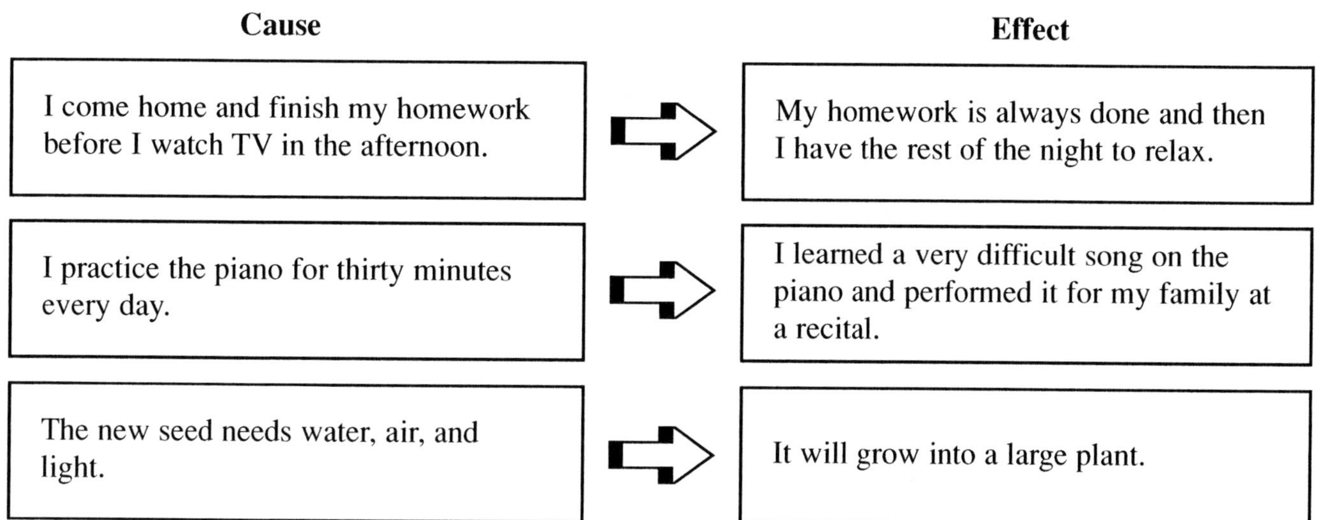

Cause
Effect
I come home and finish my homework before I watch TV in the afternoon.
My homework is always done and then I have the rest of the night to relax.
I practice the piano for thirty minutes every day.
I learned a very difficult song on the piano and performed it for my family at a recital.
The new seed needs water, air, and light.
It will grow into a large plant.

Strategy 5: If/Then Chain Reactions

Have students arrange their chairs in a large circle. Start the chain reaction by creating an if/then statement, such as: "If I go to the store, I know that I will buy some bananas." Have the next student continue by stating, "If I buy some bananas, I know I will. . . ." The chain reaction of statements continues around the circle. Finally, have them identify if/then relationships in text using the organizer on page 129.

Strategy 6: Superlative Sequence Chains

Give students several simple topics or "how-to" ideas and have them complete a sequence chain (page 130). Topics may include: brushing your teeth, making a sandwich, making an ice cream sundae, etc. Encourage students to be as detailed and specific as possible. After they share their "how-to" creations with the class, have them read sequential text and recall or identify the steps or events with great detail and precision, using another sequence chain worksheet.

Strategy 7: Making a Difference Through Community Service

Identify with students many ways that they could positively impact their school or neighborhood communities, such as cleaning up litter, planting trees in the community, or fixing playground equipment. Provide them with the Problem/Solution Organizer (page 131) or the Proposition/Support Organizer (page 132). Tell them that they need to plan out a project in which they identify a real audience, identify a problem that impacts that audience, and brainstorm solutions for the problem. Or they can make a proposal about a community problem and offer support for that proposal.

Structural Patterns

Strategy 8: Never-ending Narratives

Give students a choice of various topics that require a chronological pattern and have the first student write one sentence about one topic. (You could begin with the first or last person in each row and have him or her pass his or her paper to the student behind or in front of him or her.) Then have the next student pass his or her paper to the next student who will add the next event. Encourage students to vary their transitions, using words other than "next" and "then." Have students continue passing papers for about fifteen minutes. Stop and have some students share what has been written thus far. Ask them about the quality of the narratives and whether adding more information would improve the stories. Remind students that authors need to be judicious when adding events to stories.

Strategy 9: Time Lines

A time line helps students to show a sequence in a process or a series of events. It requires them to place one event or idea after another according to the order in which they occur. Time lines can be used in social studies to connect specific dates with events. You might have students practice with a time line by placing the events of their lives on a time line (page 133). Then they can analyze a chronological or sequential text to determine the order of important events.

Strategy 10: Structure Word Games

Divide students into groups and give them small segments of text in which the structure words have been deleted. Have them refer to the Structure Words worksheet (page 134) to identify the best words to "sew" the text back together and to help them identify the structure that the author chose to use. The simple example below demonstrates how useful this activity can be to teach students the significance of structure words.

> *A tree will undergo many changes throughout the year as the seasons change. _______________ (First), the leaves of a tree turn into brilliant colors in fall. They also begin to fall off the tree._______________ (Then) winter brings cold weather and tree limbs are bare. Most trees are without any leaves at all. _______________ (Next), springtime means that buds are growing and trees are beginning to bloom again. __________________ (Finally), summer months with lots of sunshine mean that trees continue to grow leaves and remain green. This cycle occurs each year.*

Strategy 11: Analysis of Text Structure

Collect articles, passages, or texts that are written in each of the structural patterns studied. Pair students with a partner and give each pair one type of pattern. The pair will read the text, determine the author's structure, explain how that pattern helps the author achieve his or her purpose, and then look for any flaws in the structure. Use the Analysis of Text Structure worksheet on page 135 for this activity. The partners should then report their findings to the class.

Description Tree

Directions: Identify the details in a specific text or plan your description of a topic.

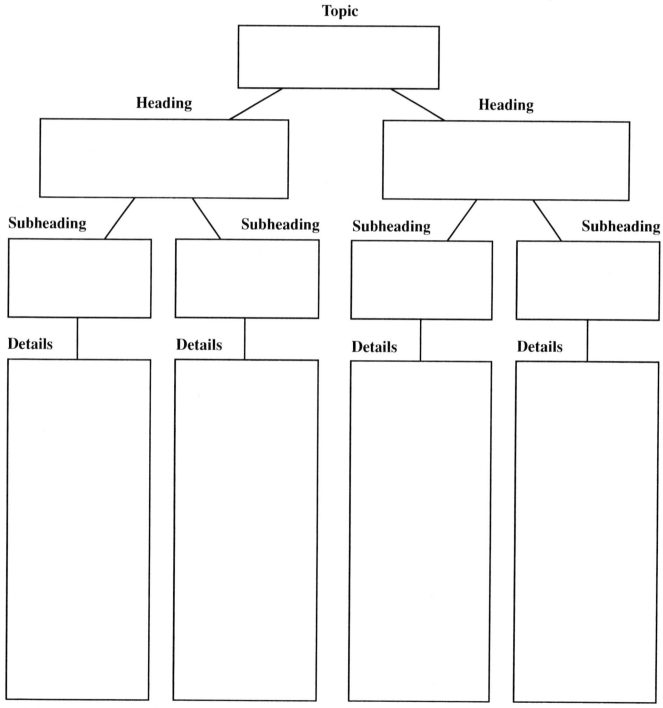

Topic

Heading

Heading

Subheading

Subheading

Subheading

Subheading

Details

Details

Details

Details

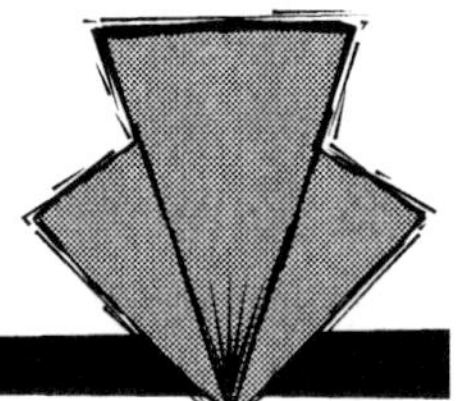

Compare/Contrast Organizer I

Directions: List similarities and differences of each of the two things being compared.

Two things being compared:

1. ______________________________

2. ______________________________

Differences	Similarities

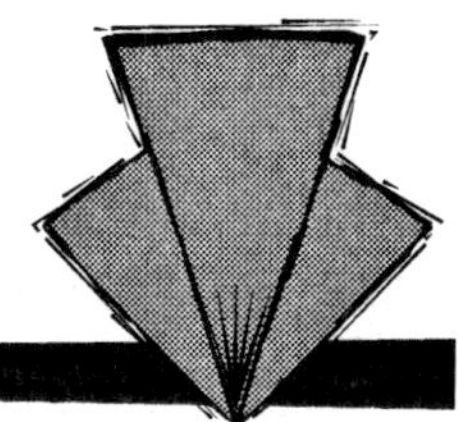

Compare/Contrast Organizer II

Directions: List the similarities and differences of each of the three things being compared.

Three things being compared:

1. ______________________________
2. ______________________________
3. ______________________________

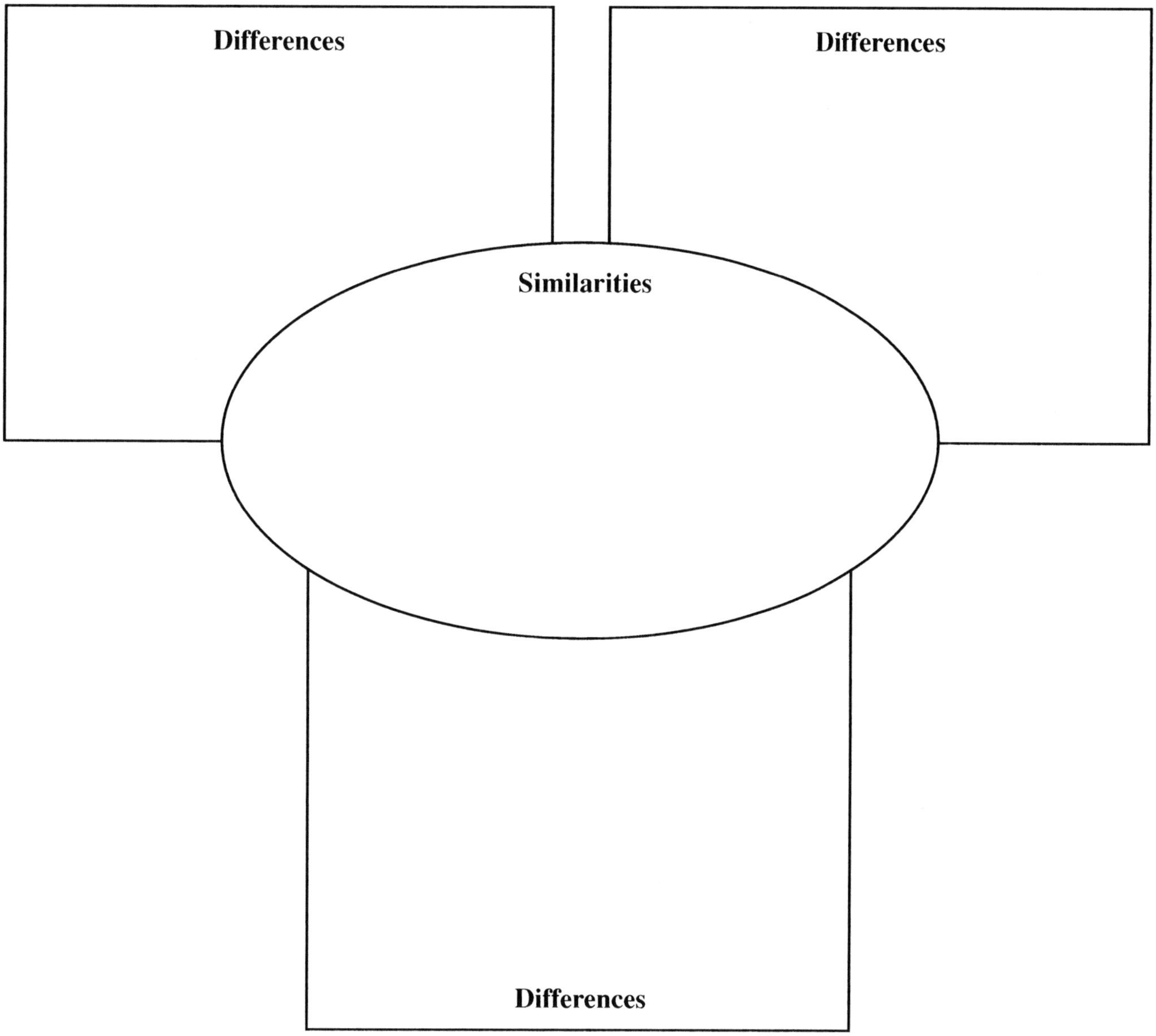

Differences

Differences

Similarities

Differences

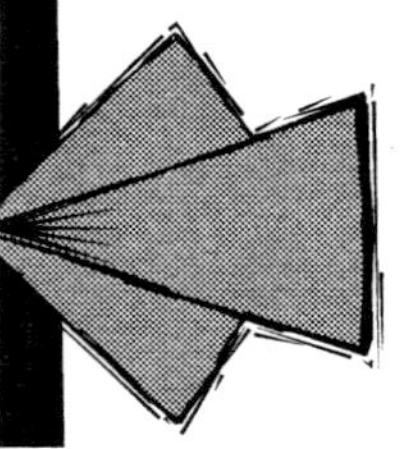

Venn Diagram

Directions: List the unique characteristics of your two topics in the outer sections of the circles. List their similar characteristics in the center section where the two circles overlap.

Differences

Similarities

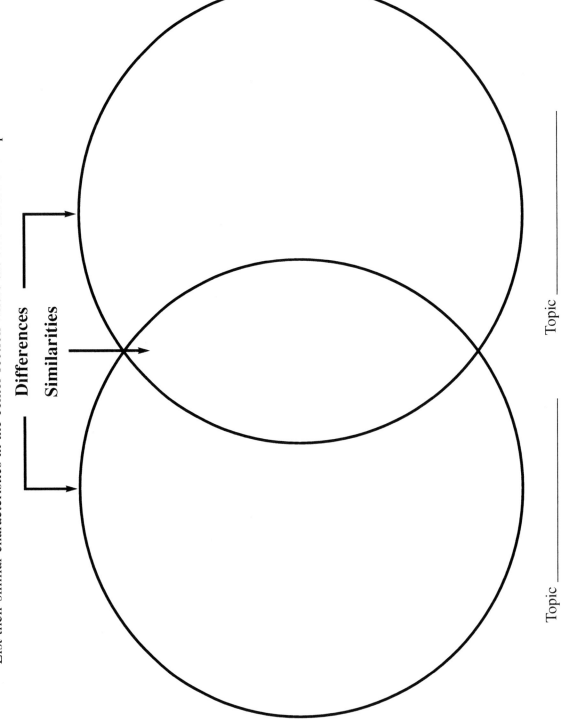

Topic ____________________

Topic ____________________

Comparison Matrix

Directions: As you read, list the features or characteristics of the topic(s) about which you are reading in the left column. Then list the things being compared across the top of the chart. Place a check in each box in which the thing being compared match the feature or characteristic listed.

Things Being Compared → **Features Used for Comparison** ↓					
1.					
2.					
3.					
4.					
5.					
6.					
7.					
8.					
9.					
10.					

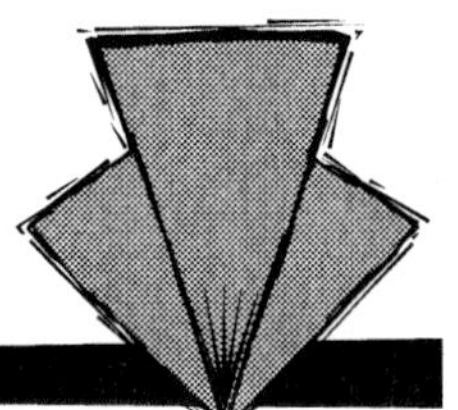

Cause-and-Effect Organizer

Cause		Effect
	⇨	
	⇨	
	⇨	

If/Then Organizer

If		Then
	⇨	
	⇨	
	⇨	

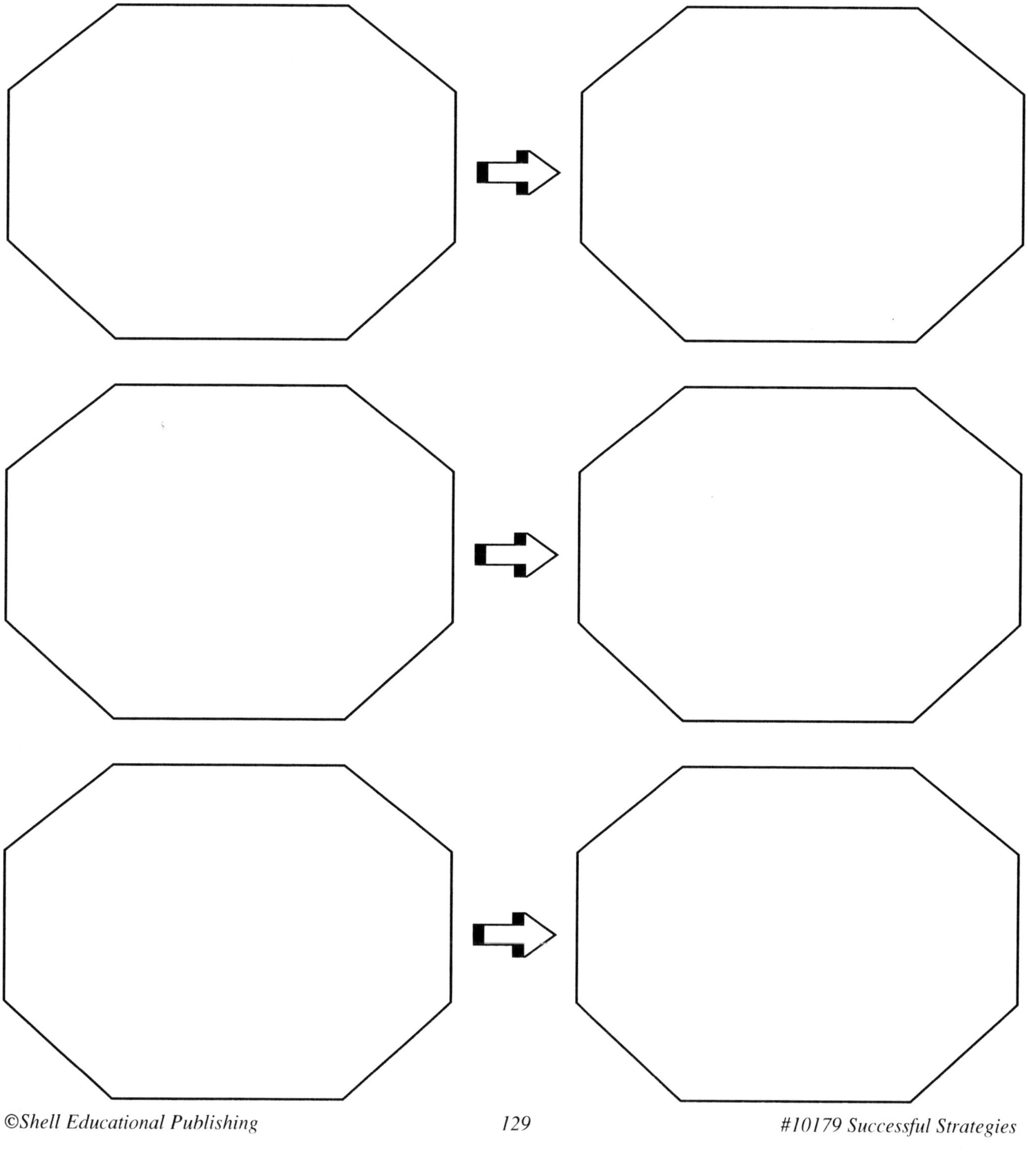

Sequence Chain

Directions: Trace the events or steps described in the text.

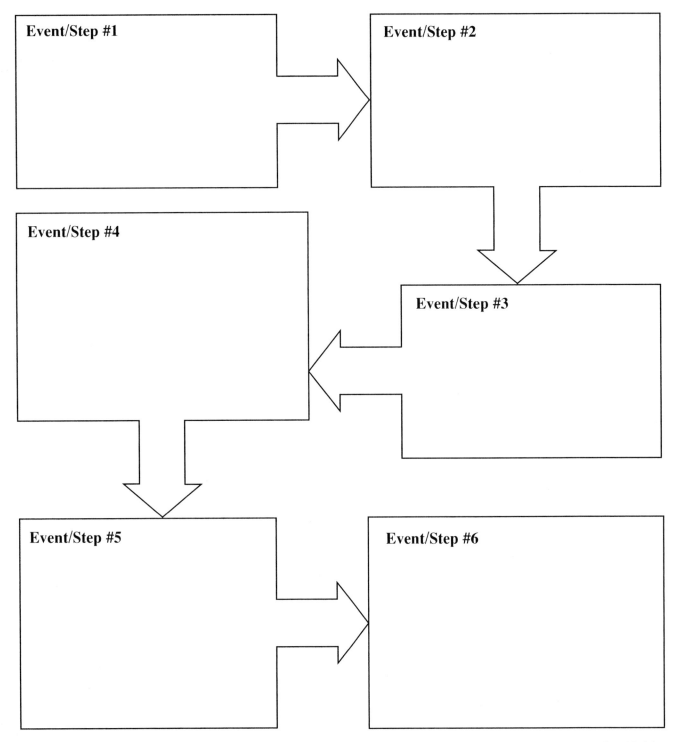

Event/Step #1

Event/Step #2

Event/Step #3

Event/Step #4

Event/Step #5

Event/Step #6

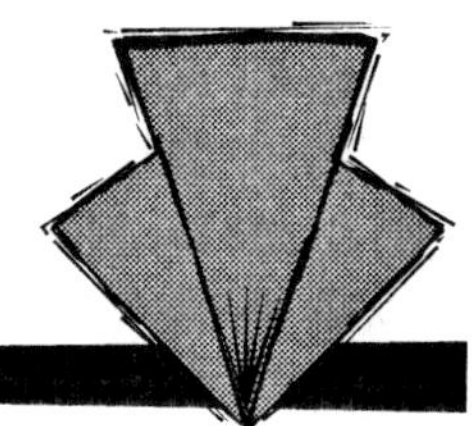

Problem/Solution Organizer

Directions: Identify the problem, solution, and pros and cons described in the text.

Problem:

Solution:

Pros	Cons

Proposition/Support Organizer

Directions: Identify the proposition, supporting details, and conclusion for your proposal or from the text.

Proposition Thesis:

Supporting Idea #1:
Supporting Idea #2:
Supporting Idea #3:

Conclusion:

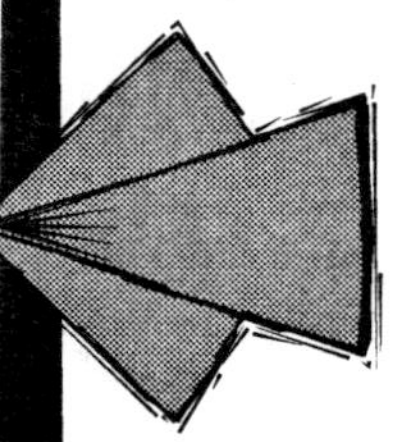

Timeline

Directions: Use this timeline to show sequence in a series of events.

____

Topic

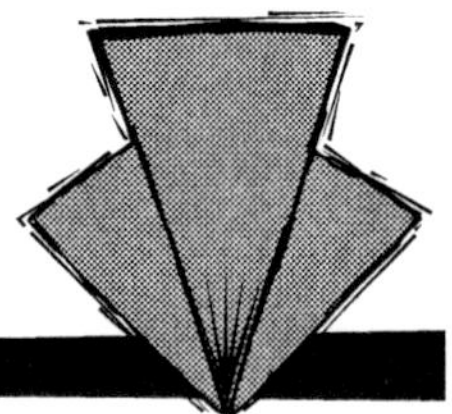

Structure Words

Directions: Use the following chart to guide you in completing the activity.

Pattern	Structure Words
Progression of ideas	for example, for instance, another, specifically, besides, also, in addition, in particular, particularly, moreover, furthermore
Cause and effect	consequently, therefore, thus, as a result, however, hence, thereby, leads to, if/then
Compare and contrast	however, on the other hand, but, by contrast, yet, unlike, like, in comparison, although, whereas, similar to, different from, similarly
Chronological, sequential	next, first, last, second, another, then, furthermore, also, additionally, in the first place, in conclusion
Proposition and support	most importantly, in support, first, next, last, in conclusion, a solution, propose

1. As you read, copy two sentences that use structure words. ______________________________

____

____

____

____

____

2. What structure is the author using? How do you know? ______________________________

____

____

____

____

____

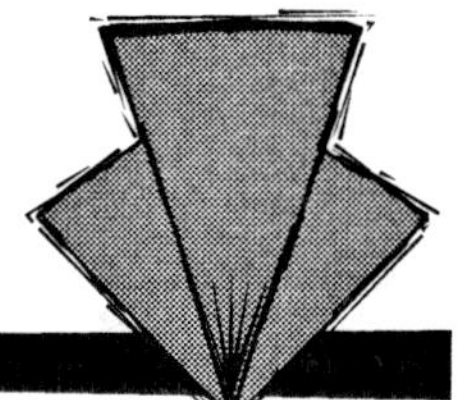

Analysis of Text Structure

Directions: Analyze the author's use of text structure.

Possible Structures

Progression of ideas
Compare and contrast
Cause and effect
Chronological, sequential
Proposition and support

1. What is the author's purpose?

____

____

____

2. Which structure is the author using? How do you know?

____

____

____

3. How does the structure help the author to achieve his or her purpose?

____

____

____

4. Are there any flaws in the structure? Explain.

____

____

____

____

____

____

____

____

Using Text Organizers

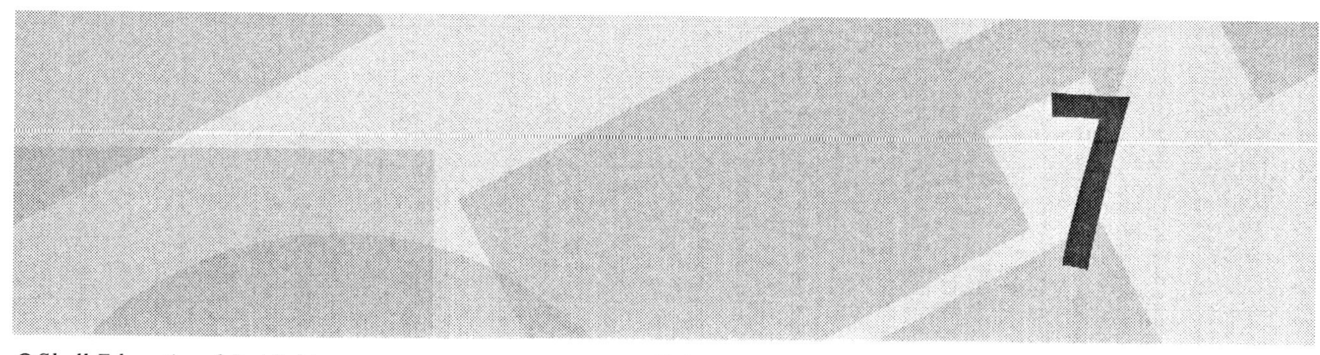

Using Text Organizers

Introduction

Text organizers are intended to enhance the text and appeal to the reader. Text organizers include chapter titles, headings and subheadings, unique typeface, graphic features, and topic and summary sentences. By the time students reach secondary school, they need to be able to evaluate whether the author's text organizers enhance or detract from the text. Such critical thinking is the foundation for high levels of reading comprehension.

Chapter Titles

Chapter titles should provide clear information regarding the main idea of the entire reading selection. These features tell the reader that this is information to take notice of. They state the main idea in just a word or a short phrase and let the reader know what information is contained in the subsequent passage. They help readers sort significant data from that which is less important. Often chapter titles are accompanied by a picture, illustration, photograph, brief explanation, or a quote that further expands the information the author wants the reader to gain. As students are reading the entire selection, they should think about how the headings, subheadings, topic and summary sentences, facts, and details all work together to support and elaborate upon the chapter title.

Using Headings and Subheadings

Informational writers organize their information under headings and subheadings. One way to help students make sense of headings and subheadings is to have them turn the information into a question and instruct them to read for the purpose of answering the question. For example, if the heading is "Photosynthesis and Its Effects on the Environment," students could convert this information into the question, "What is photosynthesis and how does it affect the environment?"

Using Text Organizers

Using Typeface

Publishers of nonfiction materials use a variety of type fonts, sizes, and effects to signal importance in a text. Typeface can be large, small, colorful, bold, italicized, squiggly, 3-D, bubbly, cartoon-like, or bulleted. Typeface may reveal importance, but it can also reveal the tone, message, or intent of the text. A change in font, bold print, or italicized words often shows the main ideas or important information. For example, a simple sentence's main idea can be changed with a change in typeface:

She did not like broccoli. (Main idea: All words are equally important.)

She did *not* like broccoli. (Main idea: Not liking broccoli is emphasized.)

She did not like *broccoli*. (Main idea: She does like other vegetables.)

Teaching students how to evaluate typeface is a critical component to helping them find important information. Some questions that may help students include:

- What inferences can you make about the topics in the text based on the style of the typeface?
- How could the typeface be improved?
- What do you think the author wants you to think or believe about the topic as result of reading the typeface?

Using Graphic Features

Illustrations, photos, diagrams, maps, tables, graphs, and charts all add meaning to a passage. They provide readers with alternative means for visualizing, mentally organizing, and remembering the information they have read. Good publishers try to present these graphic features in a colorful and visually pleasing manner to strengthen reader interest. Graphic features also enhance text through various forms of media. Magazines, advertisements, and the Internet all boast a huge variety of graphic features designed to shape and sometimes manipulate our understanding of the information. It is critical that we teach students how to evaluate which text features enhance or detract from text information. Some questions that may help students include:

- How do these graphic features help you to understand the text?
- What graphic features are missing?
- How would the addition of charts, maps, diagrams, etc., aid your understanding of the text?

Using Text Organizers

Examining Topic and Summary Sentences

Topic and summary sentences are usually generalizations that reveal the main idea at the beginning or ending of a paragraph or passage. Often the entire meaning can be gained from those two sentences alone. Understanding how authors use generalizations and specific details to construct paragraphs will help students to cognitively organize the text information. Questions to help students make sense of topic and summary sentences include:

How does the topic sentence support the main idea of the entire piece of text?

How does the summary sentence support or connect to the main idea of the entire piece of text?

What are the facts and details within the paragraph?

How do these facts and details support the topic sentence?

How do these facts and details lead to the summary sentence?

Using Strategies Independently

Secondary school readers must be adept at using text organizers to preview text, to read text comprehensively, and to review information. Model how to use text organizers for each of these purposes. Allow students to work in small groups or with partners to build their proficiency in using text organizers to make meaning of the information. Make sure that they are able to use these skills independently.

Strategy 1: Text Organizer Scavenger Hunt

Divide students into groups of four. Instruct them to use a blank sheet of paper to identify each text organizer in the chapter and whether it connects directly to the chapter title. The first group to finish wins the scavenger hunt.

Strategy 2: Chapter Challenges

Provide students with a copy of a text selection in which the title has been deleted using whiteout. Have them read the text information carefully, noting headings, subheadings, and graphic features. Challenge the class to think of as many possible chapter titles as they can. Write their suggestions on the board and have them vote on the one that seems to best represent the information in the text. Reveal the title that the author chose and ask students to determine which title best suits the text, theirs or the author's. Ask them to provide ample justification for their selection either orally or in writing. Conclude the activity by having students read the text again to complete the organizer on page 146.

Using Text Organizers

Strategy 3: Converting Headings and Subheadings into Questions

Having students convert headings and subheadings into questions is a simple way to get them to recognize the importance of these text organizers. At first, they will need your guidance in making questions. For example, if a heading is "Reptilian Habitats," some students may not automatically know to create the question, "What are reptilian habitats?" The best way to assist students is to remind them of the 5 W's + H. Then give them a number of headings and subheadings and have them convert them into questions in a whole group, with a partner, and finally on their own. The Headings and Subheadings worksheet on page 147 gives students practice in changing headings and subheadings into questions and then answering those questions.

Strategy 4: Prediction Chart

A strategy that will help students focus on the text, its organization, and what to expect is the completion of a Prediction Chart. In the first column of the chart, write in the heading of the chapter you are examining. In the second column, "My Prediction," students make predictions based on the title of that heading. Working as a whole group, brainstorm with students what a reasonable prediction would be, based on the subject of the textbook, the title of the chapter, and the title of the heading. Record this information on a transparency made from page 148 or on the board. As you are recording, be sure to ask students to tell why they would make this prediction. This provides verification of their prior knowledge, as well as leading the thought processes to other knowledge. The last column, "What Happened," is where the prediction is confirmed or disputed after they have read the text.

PREDICTION CHART (sample)

Chapter Title: Protection Against Disease

Heading Title	My Prediction	What Happened
What types of microbes are there? How do microbes spread?	It's going to tell me what microbes cause what diseases. It's going to tell me how people can get these diseases.	Viruses cause colds, chicken pox, measles, and rabies. Bacteria cause strep throat and food poisoning. Fungi cause athlete's foot and ringworm. Insects and animals, contaminated water, and spoiled or contaminated food spread disease.

Using Text Organizers

Strategy 5: Bold the "Golden" Words

Inform students that important words are boldfaced or italicized in certain kinds of text. These words are usually key terms with definitions that are critical for students to know if they are to comprehend the text. You may want to call these words the "golden" words of the text. For practice, provide students with text in which important words are not boldfaced or italicized and challenge them to underline, circle, or highlight the golden words. Have them complete the task independently and then share their text with a partner. The pairs should discuss whether each partner selected the same words. As a variation, have students write expository text about a given topic and write the "golden" key words on a separate sheet of paper. Instruct them to switch papers with a peer and have their classmate identify the key words. Have students discuss and justify their selections as a conclusion to the activity. For added practice, students can use the worksheet on page 149 to note boldfaced or italicized words, look up their meanings, and apply the words to their lives.

Strategy 6: Identifying Topic Sentences

Have students select several topic sentences from a piece of expository writing and record them on the topic sentences worksheet (page 150). Next, have them identify key words, phrases, or concepts from the topic sentences that they chose. Finally, have students create new topic sentences and experiment with capturing the key ideas and concepts in those topic sentences. As an extension, have them share their topic sentences in small groups that will choose the best one.

Strategy 7: Selecting Summary Sentences

Have students select several summary sentences from a piece of expository writing and record them on the Summary Sentences worksheet (page 151). Next, have students identify key words, phrases, or concepts from the summary sentences that they chose. Finally, have them create new summary sentences and experiment with capturing the key ideas and concepts in those sentences. As an extension, have students share their summary sentences in small groups that will choose the best one.

Using Text Organizers

Strategy 8: Evaluating Text Organizers and Graphic Features

Explicitly teaching students to evaluate text organizers is very important if students are to be critical consumers of various kinds of media. They will encounter a wide range of text organizers on the Internet and in textbooks, magazines, advertisements, and other forms of print media. Use a coding system like the one found on the worksheet (see page 152) to have students evaluate the text organizers. Have them write an explanation of the rating that they chose to give the organizer and share their justification with the whole class or with a peer. Instruct students to evaluate the color, size, content, and placement of the text organizer. Have them think about the ways in which the author or text publisher is trying to shape or manipulate their understanding of the text.

Then have students focus on the graphic features of texts, evaluating the author's choice of features. The Evaluating Graphic Features worksheet on page 153 can be used for this activity.

Strategy 9: Evaluating Author's Purpose

Thinking about the author's intent is essential for students to become critical readers. Have them use the Evaluating Author's Purpose worksheet (page 154) to identify the text organizers and determine what the author wanted them to think, feel, or believe about the topic. For example, if students are reading about westward expansion, the author may show a map of the United States with the most popular routes marked on the map. There may also be illustrations of covered wagons and other supplies that people took with them on their way west. The reader may conclude that the author wants the audience to have some sense of the distance that people traveled west, the kinds of terrain they encountered, and the crude and limited materials and supplies they possessed. The reader may determine that the author wanted him or her to understand the pioneer's experience more realistically.

Strategy 10: Choosing the Right Text Organizers

Students need to realize that too many text organizers can prove distracting and confusing to readers. Provide students with a variety of texts that have many graphic features and text organizers. Distribute the Choosing the Right Text Organizer worksheet on page 155 and have students look for those text organizers that detract from important information. They must then justify their recommendations to delete or change those text organizers. This strategy requires students to think about the importance of designing text organizers carefully.

Using Text Organizers

Strategy 11: Comparing Two Texts

Comparing texts is a good way to further extend students' abilities to think critically about text and to evaluate the effectiveness of text organizers. Pair students with a partner and provide them with at least two different texts. Distribute the Comparing Two Texts worksheet (page 156), and have the pairs use the rating system to evaluate the effectiveness of the first piece of text. They should follow the same procedure for the second text. Encourage them to think about how the color, size, placement, and content of the organizer helps or hinders their understanding of text information. Finally, have them give an overall effectiveness rating to the texts and decide which author did a better job including text organizers.

Strategy 12: Adding Text Organizers

Provide students with text that does not have any text organizers. Review the different text organizers: chapter titles, headings, subheadings, charts, diagrams, graphs, maps, illustrations, photographs, cartoons, captions, and typeface. Instruct students to find places in the text where a text organizer would really help them to understand the text better. Invite students to create a few of the text organizers for the text. If they decide to create graphs, charts, or diagrams, you may have to take them to the school library to do further research on the topic. Use the Add a Text Organizer worksheet on page 157 for this activity.

Strategy 13: Partnered Reading

Interacting with peers is an essential component for developing proficiency in reading. Students find group work highly motivating, and when it is structured, you can greatly maximize their learning. Allow students to work with a partner to complete the Partnered Reading worksheet (page 158) to identify how one text organizer reveals important information and informs the reader about the main idea and supporting details.

Strategy 14: Investigating the Internet

Having students evaluate appropriate Web sites and Web pages will help them to transfer their critical reading skills to technology. Make sure you work closely with the computer teacher or the school librarian to ensure that all sites are appropriate for students. Have students examine how the color, size, shape, movement, content, and placement of the text organizers on Web sites influence their understanding of the text information.

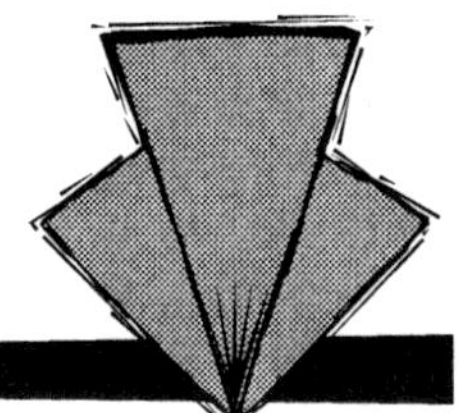

Using the Chapter Title Before, During, and After Reading

Directions: Think about the chapter title and its connection to the main ideas and supporting details of the chapter before, during, and after you read the text.

Chapter title: ____________________

Before Reading: Read the chapter title. Make a list of questions that you have about the topic in the chapter title.	**During Reading:** Take notes about the information that you are learning.
After Reading: What did you learn? Answer the questions that you asked before reading.	**Questions for Future Research:** What questions do you still have about the topic?

Headings and Subheadings

Directions: Change two of the headings or subheadings in the text into questions, answer the questions, and write a reaction to the answers.

Heading/Subheading as a Question: ____

____

Answer: ____

____

____

____

____

____

Reaction: (How does this relate to my life? What further questions do I have?) ______________

____

____

____

____

Heading/Subheading as a Question: ____

____

Answer: ____

____

____

____

____

____

Reaction: (How does this relate to my life? What further questions do I have?) ______________

____

____

____

____

Prediction Chart

Directions: Using the title and heading titles from the text, predict what the chapter will be about. Read the text and then write what happened.

Chapter Title: ______________________________

Heading Title	My Prediction	What Happened

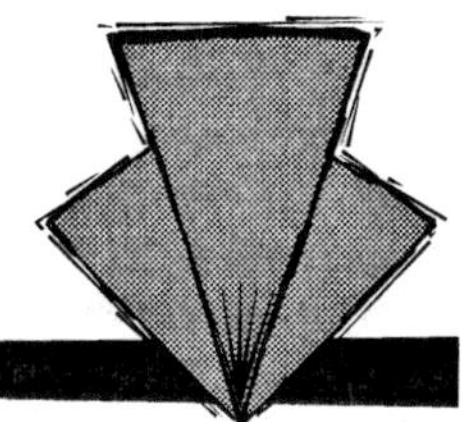

Boldfaced or Italicized Words

Directions: Define and determine the importance of boldfaced and/or italicized words. Use the glossary in the textbook or a dictionary.

Boldfaced or Italicized Word	**Definition**	**Application to Your Life:** How will you use this word in your own life? What further questions do you have about this word?

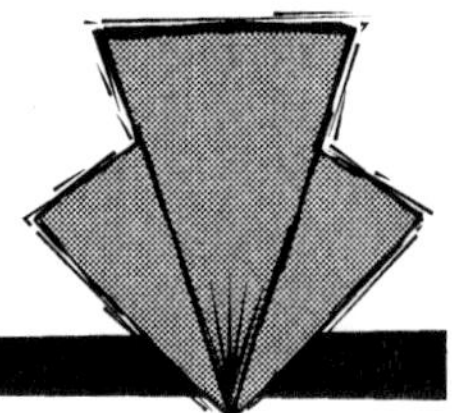

Identifying Topic Sentences

Directions: Experiment with creating new topic sentences for the text you read.

Current Topic Sentence	Key Words, Phrases, or Concepts in the Topic Sentence	New Topic Sentence

Summary Sentences

Directions: Experiment with creating new summary sentences for the text you read.

Current Summary Sentence	Key Words, Phrases, or Concepts in the Summary Sentence	New Summary Sentence

Evaluating Text Organizers

Directions: Use the following rating codes to evaluate the text organizers you encounter. Write an explanation of your rating in the chart provided below.

I = Important
LI = Limited importance
F = Flashy but not important
X = Interesting but not important

Text Organizer	Rating	Explanation

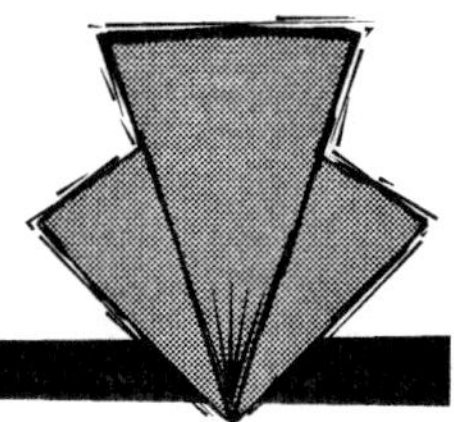

Evaluating Graphic Features

Directions: Evaluate the author's choice of graphic features.

Describe the graphic features (illustrations, photographs, captions, charts, graphs, maps, etc.)	**Evaluation** • How does this graphic feature support your understanding of the main idea and/or supporting details? • How could the graphic features have improved your understanding of the main idea and/or supporting details?

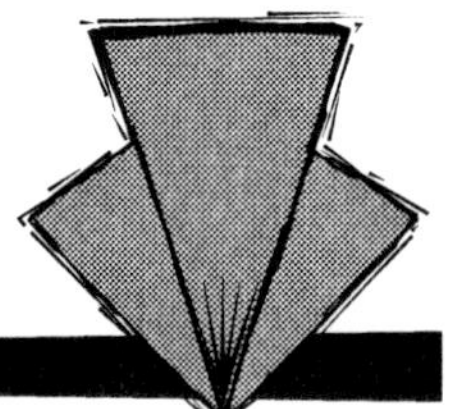

Evaluating Author s Purpose

Directions: Evaluate the author's purpose in choosing text organizers by using this chart.

Text Organizer	Inference About the Author's Purpose	Evaluation: Did the author achieve his/her purpose? Explain.

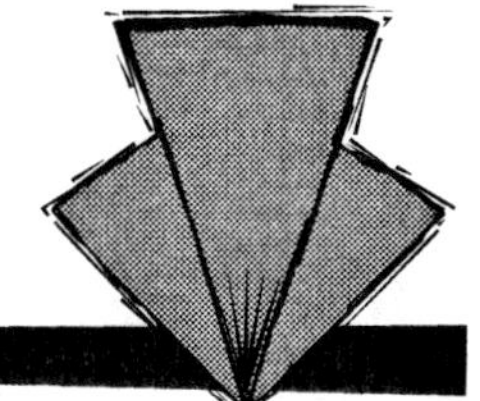

Choosing the Right Text Organizer

Directions: Read the text carefully, looking for text organizers that detract from the important information. In the chart below, write recommendations to the author in the left column and justify your recommendation in the right column.

Recommendation for Deleting or Changing a Text Organizer	Justification: Explain how this addition, deletion, or change makes the information more clear.

Why is it important for an author to design text organizers carefully? ______________________

____

____

____

____

____

____

Comparing Two Texts

Directions: Use the following chart to compare the text organizers of two different pieces of text.

Effectiveness Rating

3 = Text organizer was highly informative. It taught me a lot about the main idea.

2 = Text organizer was somewhat informative. I learned a little more about the main idea.

1 = Text organizer was not informative. I did not learn any more about the main idea.

Main Idea of Text #1	Main Idea of Text #2

Text #1		Text #2	
Text Organizers	**Effectiveness Rating**	**Text Organizers**	**Effectiveness Rating**

Overall Rating of Text #1 _________ **Overall Rating of Text #2** _________

Add a Text Organizer

Directions: Read nonfiction text that does not have any text organizers. Find the important information and record it in the left column of the chart. Then think of an illustration, chart, graph, map, or other text organizer that would enhance the text and describe or illustrate your idea.

Important Text Information	Your Idea for a Text Organizer

Using Text Organizers

Partnered Reading

Directions: With a partner, use the following worksheet to determine how text organizers reveal the main idea and supporting details of the text. Evaluate the effectiveness of the selected text organizer.

With your partner identify and describe one text organizer.	What is the main idea of the text? How do you know? Complete with your partner.
What are the details and supporting information? Complete with your partner.	How does the text organizer enhance or detract from the main idea and supporting details? Answer this question with your partner.

Using Parts of the Book

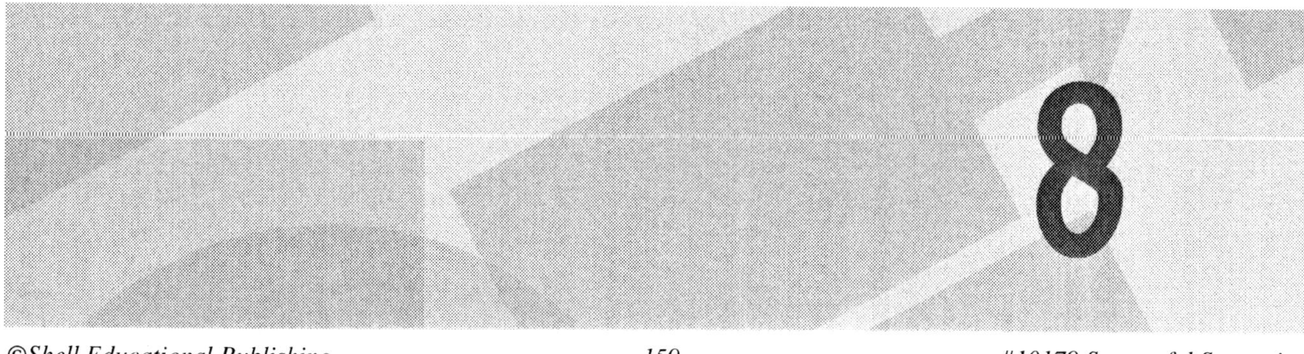

Using Parts of the Book

Introduction

Nonfiction works focus on a particular topic and are intended to provide factual information through text and visual images. Unlike fictional works that may be based on fact but are crafted through a writer's imagination, a nonfiction text must contain accurate information that is verifiable from other sources. Nonfiction texts include a variety of organizational aids such as the preface, table of contents, glossary, appendix, and index. Readers who learn to use these features will enhance their comprehension and understanding of informational texts.

- **Preface** (also known as the foreword or introduction): This section provides a lead-in for the author(s) to comment on why the book was written and provides clues as to the author's biases. This section will often contain details about the organization of the book and a suggestion about how best to read the book.

- **Table of Contents:** This provides a "road map" of what the book contains by showing how the topics in the book are grouped. It provides an efficient system to find information that is included in a general topic. Look for texts that are organized in a logical, easy-to-follow manner.

- **Glossary:** This section provides definitions of difficult terms used in the text. It is an essential aid in understanding the vocabulary of a difficult subject and a convenient aid for looking up technical and/or difficult terms.

- **Appendix:** An appendix provides additional information about a topic. It is located in the back of the book and contains information that supports and expands a chapter topic. The Appendices may also be called a "Student Almanac," "Reference," or "Reference Section."

- **Index:** This section provides the fastest means for locating topic information referred to in the text. It directs the reader to specific pages of the text.

Many times students do not need to read an entire nonfiction book to find the information they need. Knowing the parts of a book and their functions will enable students to find information and comprehend meaning more quickly. Spend time previewing the parts of each new text you give students so that they understand how it is organized.

Using Parts of the Book

Using the Preface

Understanding how to use the preface can motivate students to continue reading. When you guide students through a preview of the book, make sure to spend time skimming and scanning the preface, introduction, and/or foreword. Remind them that a preface is a preliminary statement by the author or editor of the book, setting forth its purpose and scope and sometimes expressing acknowledgment of assistance from others. Allow students opportunities to examine prefaces to see that the acknowledgement section is sometimes separate and quite extensive. Have them think about the following questions as they preview the preface:

- What did the author hope to accomplish in the preface? How do you know?
- How does the information in the preface connect to your prior knowledge on the subject?
- How could the author have improved the preface?
- Am I clear about the general topics and concepts in the book?
- Does the tone and style of the writer connect with my own tone and style?
- Will I enjoy learning this information from this author?

Using the Table of Contents

Reinforce that previewing the table of contents is one of the best tools for self-selecting a book. When students have projects in language arts or research projects across the curriculum, remind them to skim the tables of contents of several books in order to make their selections. Remind them that a table of contents is a list of the sections of the book with page numbers and that these sections may include an introduction, acknowledgments, preface, foreword, chapter titles, appendix, glossary, and index. Some questions to guide students through the previewing process include:

- How does this book or chapter connect to my assigned topic?
- Based on the title, what might I learn about the topic?
- How do these chapter titles connect to what I already know about the topic?
- How do the chapter titles build on each other?
- What will be my cumulative knowledge of the topic after reading this book?
- What chapter titles are missing? What information will I not gain from reading this book?
- Is this book worth my time? Will I achieve my purpose(s) for reading by delving into this book?

Using Parts of the Book

Using the Glossary

Reinforce that a glossary is essentially a dictionary specific to the nonfiction book they are reading. Students should know that a glossary is a readily available tool for better understanding text information. Motivated and proficient readers will often make the extra effort to seek out a dictionary to define words and terms that they do not understand. However, struggling readers will most likely not make that effort. Remind students that a glossary is a list of words with definitions intended to clarify the basic, technical, dialectical, and/or difficult terms found in the book. The glossary is usually located at the back of the book.

Using the Appendix

When students understand how to use appendices, they can gain additional and substantive information on the topics and concepts presented in the book. Review with students that an appendix is a section of materials that supplements the main text of the book and is usually placed at the end. The appendix includes examples of various portions of the text and other information that is explanatory or bibliographic. The appendix material is useful, but the book is considered complete without it. Some thought-provoking questions to share with students include:

- How does the information in the appendix add to and extend the facts and concepts that I am studying?
- What practical tips and ideas can I gain from the appendix?
- What statistical information including charts, graphs, and diagrams is included in the appendix? What kind of graphic information should be added?
- What is missing from the appendix? What would I like to know more about?
- What was the author thinking when he or she chose to include ______________ in the appendix?
- Is any part of the appendix unnecessary? How so?
- How can I use the information in the appendix to do further research?

Using Parts of the Book

Using the Index

Remind students that an index is a detailed, alphabetical key to names, places, and topics in a book including references to their page location(s). Throughout the school year, create opportunities for students to access additional information on the topics being studied by using the index. Allow them to share their thinking as they discover terms that they do not understand, find the different locations for the term, read the different explanations, and determine which explanation best matches the purpose for reading. As a variation, pair each student with a partner and have them share the responsibility for finding the term in multiple locations in the text and determining the best explanation or definition. Students will appreciate the opportunity to discuss the merits of different explanations for a word that they don't understand or about which they need more information.

Using Strategies Independently

Throughout their academic careers, students will need to be able to select nonfiction books by previewing the various parts. Secondary school readers should be proficient in using the parts of the book to make good decisions about which books will help them to meet their purpose for reading. Provide opportunities for guided practice and make sure that students get opportunities to work in small groups or with a partner to extend their use of previewing strategies. Build their confidence through praise and encouragement when they make wise book selections. Reinforce students' skills by requiring them to justify why they chose the book(s) that they did.

Strategy 1: Previewing the Preface

Have students identify their purpose for reading, allow them to read the preface or introduction, and help them through discussion to understand the author's purpose for writing. Instruct them to use the Previewing the Preface worksheet (page 169) to identify the background of the book, the major topics to be covered, and the tone. Then they decide whether they should keep on reading.

Strategy 2: Using the Foreword

Once students have identified their purpose for reading, have them complete the Using the Foreword worksheet (page 170) to identify key words and phrases, to make a prediction about what they will learn, and to explain how the information connects to their prior knowledge and purpose for reading. Then they should ask any further questions that they have about the topic. Emphasize to students that the foreword, preface, and/or introduction all provide critical information to the reader that becomes the foundation for deciding whether or not to keep reading.

Using Parts of the Book

Strategy 3: Table of Contents Questions

Have students use the worksheet entitled Table of Contents Questions (page 171) to convert each of the chapter titles into a question. Then have them read the chapter and record a general answer to the question. Finally, have students identify at least one additional question they have about the topic in the chapter. The example below shows how students might look at a table of contents and turn each title into a question to try to answer as they read.

Holiday Traditions Around the World

Table of Contents

Chapter Titles Converted to Questions

Do all countries celebrate New Year's Day on the same day?

What is Carnival? What countries celebrate that day?

What are the traditions of Passover?

How do we know that July 4th is our Independence Day?

What language is Dia de los Muertos? What does it mean?

What kinds of festivals happen in winter? Do they use a kind of light?

What is Boxing Day and where is it celebrated?

Using Parts of the Book

Strategy 4: Using a Glossary

Begin by informing students that some nonfiction books have a built-in dictionary called a glossary. As they read the text, have them identify words with which they are not familiar by recording them on the Using a Glossary worksheet (page 172). Have students look up the words in the glossary and record the definitions on the worksheet. Finally, have them reflect on how the definition helps to clarify their understanding of the text information. As a variation, have students create an illustrated mini-glossary (page 173). Have students read a short piece of nonfiction text, identify terms with which they are not familiar, use the dictionary to create a short definition, and design a simple illustration or symbol to represent the newly learned word. Using art is always motivating to students and will reinforce their understanding of the glossary.

Strategy 5: The Appendix

Guide students in identifying their purpose for reading and allow them to select a nonfiction book to meet that purpose. Provide them with The Appendix worksheet (page 174) and have them select five topics from the appendix that match their purpose for reading (or simply look interesting). Have them record the topics, page numbers, and definitions or key words in the chart. Allow students to work with a partner to complete this activity. Then, have the pairs preview the rest of the book to determine information that might be missing from the appendix. Instruct them to discuss and describe an addition to the appendix that they could create.

Strategy 6: Investigating the Index

Lead students to an understanding of their purpose for reading. Then, have them use the Investigating the Index worksheet (page 175) to record unfamiliar words or terms. Instruct students to use the index to locate additional sources of information from throughout the book and record the page numbers on the worksheet. Finally, after students have investigated each of the identified page numbers, have them reflect on the information that they found most useful. This information can be in the form of facts, details, examples, illustrations, charts, graphs, etc. Allow for the possibility that none of the additional places in the text were useful. Encourage students to discuss the remaining questions they have as well as strategies for finding the information they need.

Using Parts of the Book

Strategy 7: Team Book Investigation

Divide students into groups of four and have them work with their group to answer the questions on the Team Book Investigation worksheet (page 176). As students work together, they will be thinking about how the preface, table of contents, index, and appendix help them to achieve their purpose for reading. Have them examine different books and communicate their findings to the class.

Strategy 8: Evaluating the Parts of a Nonfiction Book

Take students to the school library to select a book or have them choose one from the classroom library. Make sure to identify the purpose for reading or guide students in identifying their own purpose for reading. Provide them with the worksheet entitled Evaluating the Parts of a Nonfiction Book (page 177). Have them record the parts of the book; make observations about the content of the book by commenting on facts, details, length, attractiveness, and author's purpose; and finally, evaluate the usefulness of each part of the book by reflecting on their purpose for reading.

Strategy 9: Text Coding

Marking the text is a great monitoring tool for students to use in order to ensure that they are meeting their purpose for reading. Present students with three codes: **C** to represent the concept they are studying; **M** to represent what further information they need; and **?** to represent the information that they do not understand. Instruct them to mark directly in the text, if they can, use sticky notes, or create a bookmark on which to record the codes. When they are finished reading and marking text, have them record the corresponding text information on the Text Coding worksheet (page 178). Then have them identify the part of the book that they think will be the most useful in finding more information or clarifying their confusion. Finally, instruct students to identify the information that they found.

Text Coding

C — Concept being studied

M — More information needed

? — Information not understood

Using Parts of the Book

Strategy 10: Analyzing the Author's Choices

Being critical of the author's choices is an important skill that proficient readers possess. Have students use the Analyzing the Author's Choices worksheet (page 179) to identify the major components of the nonfiction book. Then, have them evaluate the author by deciding through careful examination whether each of these parts is comprehensive, attractive, helpful, interesting, organized, and connected to the main idea(s) of the book. Encourage students to elaborate using adequate examples and offer suggestions about the revisions that the author should make. You may need to model this evaluation for students depending on their maturity and skill levels.

Strategy 11: Locating Information with a Partner

Students can use the Locating Information with a Partner worksheet on page 180 to work in pairs to find information in various parts of a book. The pairs can determine a topic of study and then determine the best place in the book to find the needed information.

Previewing the Preface

Directions: Analyze the preface of the nonfiction book.

Definition of the preface: a preliminary statement by the author or editor of a book, setting forth its purpose and scope, expressing acknowledgment of assistance from others

Purpose for reading: ________________________________

Author's purpose: ________________________________

Description of the background of the book (may include where the idea of the book came from):

____

____

____

____

____

____

____

What are the major topics covered in the book (scope)? ________________________________

____

____

____

What is the tone of the book (formal/informal; informative/entertaining; chatty/serious, etc.)? Explain.

____

____

____

____

Will you keep reading based on the preface? Explain. ________________________________

____

____

Using the Foreword

Directions: Analyze the foreword of a nonfiction text.

Definition of the foreword: an introduction or preface to the book

Purpose for reading: ____

____

What are the key words or phrases from the foreword?	What do you predict that you will learn?
How will this information connect to your prior knowledge and/or your purpose for reading?	What questions do you have about the topic based on the foreword?

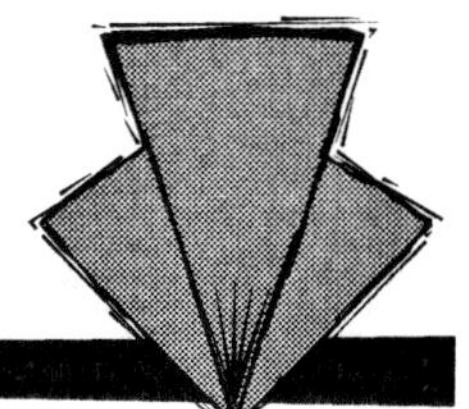

Table of Contents Questions

Directions: Change the chapter titles to questions, record a general answer, and generate a new question about the contents of the chapter.

Definition of the table of contents: a list of the sections of the book with page numbers (sections include: introduction, acknowledgments, preface, foreword, chapter titles, appendix, glossary, index,

Chapter Title	Convert Chapter Title to a Question	General Answer	A New Question

Using a Glossary

Directions: As you read, record words with which you are unfamiliar. Look up these words in the glossary and record the definition in your own words. Then, identify how the definition helped you to clarify the text information.

Definition of a glossary: a list of words with definitions intended to clarify the basic, technical, dialectical, and/or difficult terms found in the book

Terms/words with which you are unfamiliar	Definition in your own words	How does this definition help to clarify your understanding of the text information? How does this definition connect to what you are learning in the classroom?

Creating an Illustrated Mini-Glossary

Directions: Create an illustrated mini-glossary that will help the reader understand the text information. As you read, highlight or underline words that you do not understand. Then record the words below, look them up in a dictionary and restate the definition in a simpler way in your own words. Finally, create an illustration or symbol to represent the word.

Term/Word	Brief Definition	Illustration/Symbol

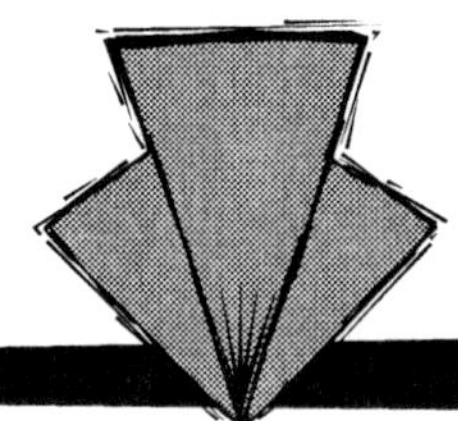

The Appendix

Directions: Identify your purpose for reading, select a nonfiction book, and then preview the appendix. Select five topics that match your purpose. Record the topics and the page number in the chart. Then look up each topic and record the definition or key words and phrases about the topic.

Definition of an appendix: A section of materials that supplements the main text of the book and is usually placed at the end. The appendix includes examples of various portions of the text and other information that is explanatory or bibliographic. The appendix material is useful, but the book is considered complete without it.

Purpose for reading: ____

____

Topic	Page Number	Definition or Key Words and Phrases from the Text to Describe the Topic

Investigating the Index

Directions: Identify your purpose for reading. As you read, record unfamiliar words or terms. Use the index to locate additional sources of information. Record the facts, details, and examples in the book that best helped you to understand the unfamiliar word or term and achieve your purpose for reading.

Definition of an index: a detailed alphabetical key to names, places, and topics in a book including references to their page location(s)

Purpose for reading: ____

____

Unfamiliar word or term	Page numbers where additional information can be found	Information that is most useful (details, facts, examples) Further questions about the term

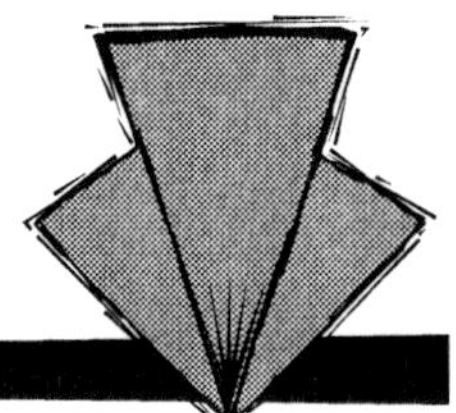

Team Book Investigation

Directions: In your group of four, assign each member a question to answer. Record your answers in the boxes below.

Purpose for reading: ____

____

What information from the preface will help us to achieve our purpose?	How will the table of contents help us to achieve our purpose?
What information from the appendix will be helpful?	How will the index help us to achieve our purpose?

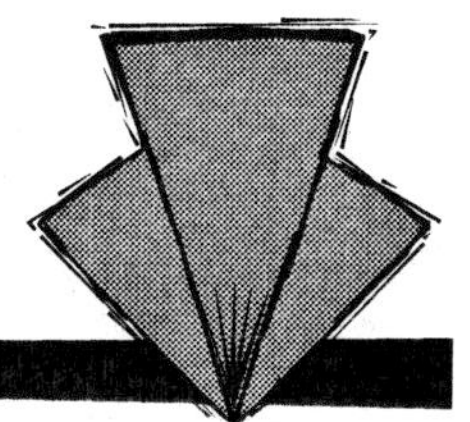

Evaluating the Parts of a Nonfiction Book

Directions: Begin by identifying your purpose for reading. Then identify the parts of the nonfiction book you have chosen, make observations about the content, and evaluate the usefulness of that part. Use the "Usefulness categories" to make your prediction.

Purpose for reading: ______________________________

____

Possible parts of a nonfiction book: preface, foreword, introduction, acknowledgments, table of contents, chapters, index, glossary, and appendix

Usefulness categories:
- Highly useful
- Somewhat useful
- Not very useful

Part of the book	Observations about content (facts, details, length, attractiveness, author's purpose, etc.)	Prediction about usefulness in terms of meeting your purpose

Text Coding

Directions: As you are reading, use the codes to mark the text. If you cannot write on the text, use sticky notes, or make a little book mark and line it up with the text and mark your codes. When you are finished, fill in the chart below. Record the text information that you found in the left column and the section(s) of the nonfiction book that you think will help you the most in the center column. Finally, use the right column to record the information that you found.

C = How does this idea **connect** to the concept I am studying?

M = I'd like to know **more** about this topic.

? = **I don't understand** this information.

Possible parts of a nonfiction book: preface, foreword, introduction, acknowledgments, table of

Text information (what you want to know more about or your question regarding the information you don't understand)	**Section of the book you think will be most useful**	**What you found**

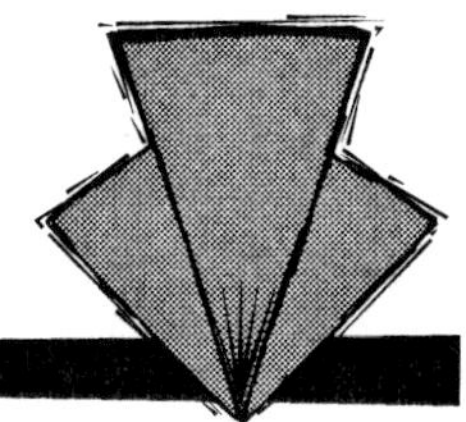

Analyzing the Author s Choices

Directions: Evaluate the contents of each of the parts of the nonfiction book identified on the left.

Part of the nonfiction book	**Analysis:** Is this part comprehensive? Attractive? Helpful? Interesting? Connected to the main idea of the book? Organized? Explain your answer fully. Be sure to offer suggestions about what the author could improve, add, change, or delete.
Preface, Foreward, or Introduction	
Table of Contents	
Glossary	
Appendix	
Index	

Locating Information with a Partner

Directions: Locate information with a partner.

Possible parts of a nonfiction book: preface, foreword, introduction, acknowledgments, table of contents, chapters, index, glossary, and appendix

Topic: ____________________

What questions do we have about the topic? What do we want to know more about?	What information did we find to answer our questions? What further questions do we have?
Did the author do a good job including necessary parts of the book in order to assist the reader?	Which part of the book was most useful in finding answers to our questions?

Making Inferences

Making Inferences

Introduction

To gain meaning from text, students must be able to infer. Inference is the process of judging, concluding, or reasoning based on given information. Strategies for inferring are closely related to those used for visualizing. While visualizing involves mental images, inferring has to do with words and thoughts; when used together, inferring and visualizing strengthen understanding.

The process of inferring involves reader interpretation of the text. A capable reader will work hard to discover the meaning of unclear words, terms, or concepts and connect them to the rest of the text. He or she will make defensible inferences that will explain the problems, places, or information in the text, using appropriate examples such as quotes, facts, evidence, and sources. In other words, a good reader will use good sources and/or quotes to support inferences and opinions. Perhaps most importantly, the capable reader will connect his or her inferences to the overall main idea or historical or cultural perspective.

Raising Questions

An effective method for increasing students' inferencing skills is to ask many questions. Questions should be both **text explicit** and **text implicit**, but text implicit questions are the ones that require inferential, divergent thinking.

Text explicit questions are those questions where students can find the answer directly from the reading. No inference is required to arrive at an answer. Text explicit comprehension requires the reader to read the lines and state what the author of the text says. There is typically only one correct answer to text explicit questions.

On the other hand, **text implicit** questions require the reader to combine what is read with other information based on prior knowledge and experience. The reader must read between the lines, and there are usually several plausible answers. Additionally, asking questions that require students to think on their own and to go beyond the text is the highest level of questioning.

When formulating questions from a particular text, focus on important aspects of the reading. Questions that are created to promote effective interactions with text will help to avoid focusing on trivial facts and will get right to the heart of the reading goals. Using question stems that move through Bloom's Taxonomy (pages 189 and 190) will take the students from text explicit to text implicit and will assist students in gaining a more meaningful understanding of the material.

Teachers will need to teach questioning skills in order for struggling readers to learn how to raise questions and find answers. Additionally, proficient readers will need guided practice to strengthen their existing questioning skills. When readers ask questions, such as, "How does my prior knowledge help me to understand the text?" and "How does using my visualization techniques help me to create a complete picture of what's going on in the text?" their ability to make inferences develops.

Making Inferences

Making Observations

Proficient readers make observations about text features, text content, and the author's choices. Insightful observations provide the groundwork for conclusions and inferences. For example, when a reader can identify specific aspects of a text feature, the likelihood of making critical inferences about the connection between the text feature and the author's purpose is greatly increased. Some ways to increase students' observational skills include teaching students how to:

- skim and scan for specific text features or specific content
- read silently and generate questions
- read with a partner and generate questions
- pause during reading to respond, react, and reflect
- reread for clarification

Making, Confirming, and Revising Predictions

Before students read, they must be able to make predictions about the information they are about to learn. To make predictions, they need to preview the text and infer what the author wants them to learn. Then while students read, they need to think about their earlier predictions for the purpose of confirming or contradicting their initial thinking. As they continue the process of reading and when they are finished reading, they need to revisit and revise their earlier predictions and examine how the author was shaping the information in order to create their final understanding of the text. Students need to be able to predict the overall meaning of the text and how they will use the information once they are finished reading. They need to be able to draw inferences and predict outcomes. For example, if students are reading about the court cases, *Brown vs. the Board of Education* or *Plessy vs. Ferguson,* they need to think how these cases connect to the concept of civil rights that they are studying. By drawing inferences about this connection to the civil rights movement, they will be able to predict what they will need to do with the information once they are finished reading.

Making Inferences

Making Interpretations

When students make interpretations about text meaning, they are tapping into higher order thinking skills. Questioning, visualizing, and inferencing are developmental processes that aid readers in deepening their interpretations of the text. Proficient readers will examine cause-and-effect relationships, compare-and-contrast information, and engage in problem-solving techniques to gain more from the text than what is merely on the page. Some readers believe that nonfiction text simply contains information to be learned. It is important to convey the importance of interpreting nonfiction text and to dispel the notion that the information is simply to be acquired. Students need to be able to evaluate the author's message, understand how their beliefs and attitudes about the topic are being shaped, and connect the text information with what they have already learned about the topic.

Conveying Underlying Meanings

It is important that secondary school readers be able to identify and convey the underlying meaning in text. Often authors weave their bias throughout the text in such subtle ways that it is difficult for even the most astute reader to identify their intentions. The following questions will help students identify the underlying meaning in the text:

- What does the author believe about the topic? How do you know?
- What does the author want you to learn from this article?

Give students multiple opportunities to convey text meanings to other students. Also provide them with opportunities to generate their own expository writing and evaluate it for underlying meaning. The Conveying Underlying Meanings worksheet on page 191 gives students practice in discovering meaning.

Making Speculations

Speculating about future events in the text, their implications for the reader, and the importance of text information helps readers to build the foundation for drawing conclusions and inferencing. When students wonder about the text, they:

- create mental images in order to develop a clearer picture of the text
- link personal experience and prior knowledge to the text
- develop deeper levels of comprehension
- gain an increased appreciation for reading

Making Inferences

Reacting

While proficient readers react to text in a variety of ways, struggling readers do not have a mental "tool box" to use to respond to text by inferencing and drawing conclusions. Students need to be taught how to identify important text information, choose a method for reacting, and link prior knowledge and personal experience to the text.

Identifying and Assessing Evidence

An effective way to teach students to identify and assess evidence is to present them with a question that requires them to read to answer the question. Then require them to gather text evidence to support the answer to the question; and show them how to assess the validity of the information, the credibility of the sources, and comprehensiveness of the information.

Using Strategies Independently

One of the best ways to develop student proficiency is to allow them to work in groups to practice strategies. Socialization is highly motivating to students and is an excellent vehicle for providing guided practice toward mastery. Some tips for supporting group work include:

- Provide step-by-step directions about what you expect from students.
- Assign roles and responsibilities to each group member.
- Require students to "publish" their work, either through oral sharing or a written assignment that will be posted in the classroom.

Once students have had exposure to group work, make sure to provide them opportunities to use the skills that they have learned independently.

Strategy 1: Inferencing About the Author

Begin by having students read the text and identify important events. Instruct them to use the Inferencing About the Author worksheet (page 192) to record relevant text information. Have them use the right side of the double-entry journal to reflect on what the author wants them to learn, what the author believes about the subject, and whether or not they share the author's beliefs. The worksheet on page 193 can also help them infer the author's intent.

Making Inferences

Strategy 2: Text on the Page/Text in My Head

One of the goals of sound reading instruction is that students understand that the words on the page do not hold all of the meaning of the text. Have them use the worksheet (page 194) to record the specific information from the text on the left, and the "text in their heads" on the right side of the journal. Students must learn that the text in their heads is a compilation of the all the prior knowledge and personal experiences that they bring to their reading experiences.

Strategy 3: Text Coding

Providing students with a text coding system can be a highly effective way for them to keep track of important text information that they would like to revisit. Have them use the text coding worksheet (page 195) to record text information that corresponds with the coding that they used to mark the text itself or on a sticky note. Then, have them write a detailed response or explanation that demonstrates their ability to infer, predict, draw a conclusion, question, or make connections to prior knowledge.

Strategy 4: Conceptual Inferencing

Using concept-based principles is the most highly effective way to help students retain factual information. Make sure to identify the concept that you want students to learn throughout the course of the unit. Present them with guiding questions that will help them to categorize and make sense of the vast amounts of information they will be learning. Give them the Conceptual Inferencing guide worksheet (page 196) and have them record facts from the text on the left and their inferences on the right.

Strategy 5: Global Inferencing

Have students use the Global Inferencing worksheet (page 197) to make inferences about people, events, settings, and other important facts in the text. Instruct students to make a connection to the concept being studied and the guiding questions they are investigating. Consider dividing students into groups of four and having each member take the responsibility for one of the boxes in the global inferencing strategy.

Making Inferences

Strategy 6: Insightful Interpretations

Begin by providing students with a purpose for reading. You may want to remind them of the concept they are studying and refer them to guiding questions. Give students the Insightful Interpretations worksheet (page 198), and have them record significant text information and their own inferences about the text. Then have them discuss their observations with a partner and record his or her inferences. Give students an opportunity to read about the topic from another source and make an inference. Finally, share your inferential interpretation of the text.

Strategy 7: Partnered Reading

Provide students with sentence starters in order to guide them with Partnered Reading worksheet (page 199). Give them an opportunity to read together and record significant text information and related inferences. Have students highlight and discuss the similarities and differences between their inferences.

Strategy 8: Perceptive Predictions

Have students read a persuasive piece of text. Instruct them to complete the Perceptive Predictions worksheet (page 200) and identify the issue, solution, and pros and cons of the topic presented in the article. Finally, have students identify the author's beliefs about the topic and what the author expects the reader to do with the information.

Strategy 9: Text Feature Inferencing

Before reading, review with students the concept being learned and the guiding questions. Preview the text by asking students about the text features and their possible connections to the topic and concept they are learning. As students are reading, have them record their observations about the text features using the Text Feature Inferencing worksheet (page 201). Then have them make inferences about the text features' connections to the major concept being studied.

Strategy 10: Artistic Inferencing

Provide students with the Artistic Inferencing worksheet (see page 202). Then have them draw an illustration of the concept or topic. You will find that students will combine the information from the text itself and the "text in their heads" to create their illustrations. Instruct students to reflect on their illustrations and make observations about the details, colors, and ideas that were from their prior knowledge about the topic.

Making Inferences

Bloom's Taxonomy

Bloom's Taxonomy is a classification system that uses educational objectives for developing higher-level thinking skills. In order to meet the needs of a variety of learners, teachers can utilize this model to present ideas and concepts at many different levels. When writing your own questions, include at least one question from each level.

1. **Knowledge**

   Recall, remember, memorize, or recognize information. This is the basic level that establishes a foundation for better understanding. Tasks include asking students to define, describe, label, locate, recite, select, memorize, recognize, name, state, identify, repeat, and list.

2. **Comprehension**

   This requires students to understand information and the focus is on the meaning and intent of the reading material. This level requires a translation of data from one form to another. When students are asked to restate, paraphrase, rewrite, convert, give examples, illustrate, summarize, explain, and locate, they are working at the comprehension level.

3. **Application**

   At this level, problem solving is required. Students use the information in the material to transfer their learning to new and concrete situations. Verbs to use in application questions include apply, modify, dramatize, translate, demonstrate, and construct.

4. **Analysis**

   Students examine specific parts of information to identify the underlying ideas. It is a strategy that is utilized when attacking a problem or reaching a decision. Tasks include asking students to analyze, classify, distinguish, subdivide, separate, differentiate, examine, calculate, compare, and contrast.

5. **Synthesis**

   Something fresh and different is done with the information; parts and elements of the material are put together in a new form. Verbs to use in synthesis questions include combine, compose, design, organize, invent, develop, plan, create, and devise.

6. **Evaluation**

   The highest level of the taxonomy, this requires assessment of the quality or judgment of the value of material based on internal evidence (logic) or external criteria or standard. Include words such as evaluate, recommend, summarize, debate, criticize, or judge.

Making Inferences

Bloom's Taxonomy Question Stems

Consider students' level of cognitive development according to Bloom's Taxonomy. Then use these stems to develop questions and prompts that will match their needs.

Knowledge

1. Who?
2. What?
3. When?
4. Where?
5. How?
6. List the facts in order.

Comprehension

1. What is meant by. . .?
2. Can you describe. . .?
3. What is the difference. . .?
4. What is the main idea. . .?
5. Why does. . .?
6. Explain why. . . .

Application

1. Who would you choose. . .?
2. What would happen if. . .?
3. How would you. . .?
4. Do you know someone like. . .?
5. Would you do the same thing in the same situation?
6. If you had to. . ., what would you do?

Analysis

1. What part of the reading is the funniest?
2. What part is the most exciting?
3. What part is the saddest?
4. Which things are facts and which are opinions?
5. What can you do that is just like what the person in the story does?
6. List five compound words from the story.
7. What is the purpose of…?

Synthesis

1. Retell one event from an animal's point of view.
2. How could we/you…?
3. Make up another ending for the story that still fits the details.
4. Rewrite a sentence from the reading but change one thing in it.
5. Write a new title for this story.
6. Write a six-line rhyming poem about the reading.

Evaluation

1. Is the main character in this reading good or bad? Why?
2. Which is better, . . .?
3. Would you agree that. . .?
4. What is your opinion of. . .?
5. Are they right to do. . .? Why or why not?
6. Compare two characters in the reading. Tell which one you think is better and why.

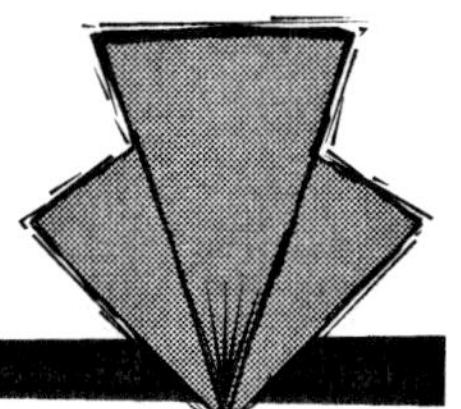

Conveying Underlying Meanings

Directions: Convey underlying meanings about the topic you read.

Underlying Meaning: the author's hidden intent; information that you have to infer

Topic or Concept: ______________________________

Important Text Information	**Key Words, Phrases, or Concepts** (context clues that help you to infer the underlying meaning)	**Underlying Meaning**

Inferencing About the Author

Directions: Record text information on the left side and inferences about the author on the right side.

Text Information	Inferencing
What is happening in the text? What events have occurred?	What does the author want me to learn from this? What does the author believe about the topic? Do I share the author's beliefs? Is the author making an impact on me?

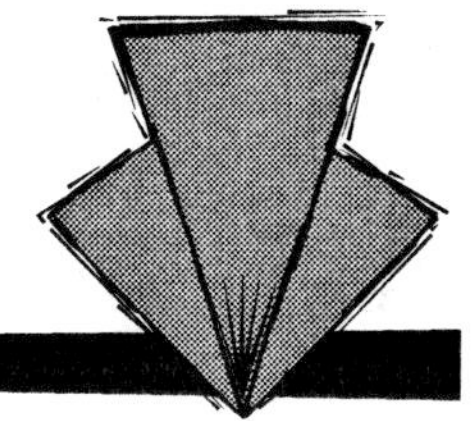

Inferring the Author s Intent

Directions: Respond to the prompts and questions in order to draw a conclusion about the author's intent.

Title of text: ______________________________

Main topic: ______________________________

Important subtopics: ______________________________

____

____

Text structure selected: ______________________________

Text features included: ______________________________

____

Words or phrases that reveal the author's beliefs or opinions about the topic:

____

____

____

Conclusion about the author's purpose (What does the author want the reader to gain from reading the information?):

____

____

____

____

____

____

____

____

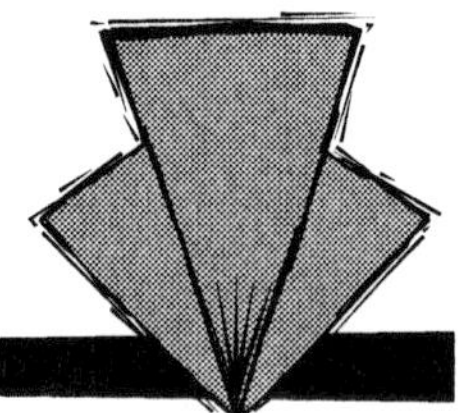

Identifying the Text in My Head

Directions: Record significant information from the text on the left side of the double-entry journal. On the right side, record images, thoughts, and ideas from your own background knowledge as well as inferences about the topic and text.

The Text on the Page	The Text in My Head

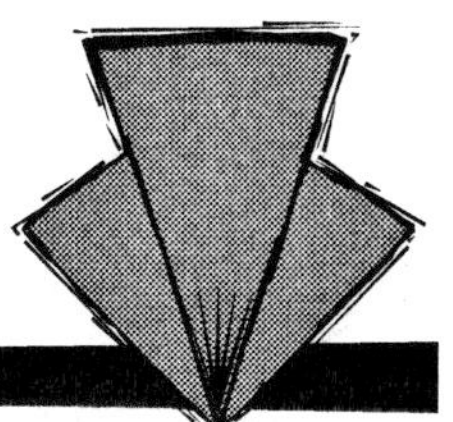

Text Coding for Inferential Thinking

Directions: As you read, use the codes to mark in the margins or on a sticky note next to significant segments of text. Then use the chart to record the text information connected to the code in the left column of the chart and a response in the right column of the chart.

I = Inference
P = Prediction
C = Conclusion
? = I wonder
PK = Prior knowledge connection

Text Information	**Response or Explanation** (Remember that you are making an inference or prediction, drawing a conclusion, wondering about the text, or connecting to prior knowledge.)

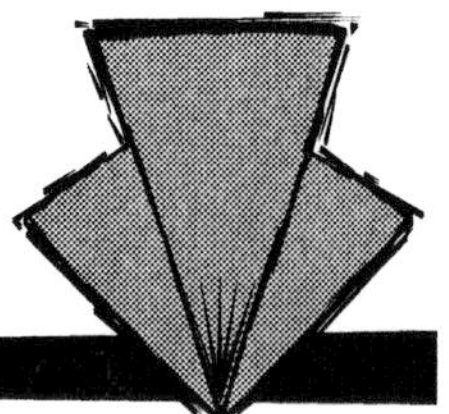

Conceptual Inferencing

Directions: Make inferences about the facts you are learning and their connection to the larger concept.

Concept Being Studied: ____

Guiding Questions: ____

____

Facts from the Text	**Inferences** (How do these facts connect to the larger concept? How do these facts help you to answer the guiding questions?)

Global Inferencing

Directions: Make inferences about people, settings, events, and other related facts in the text.

Concept Being Studied: ______________________________

Guiding Questions: ______________________________

____

People in the Text	Settings in the Text
Inferences about connection to concept:	Text support or prior knowledge support:
Inferences about connection to concept:	Text support or prior knowledge support:
Events in the Text	**Other Related Facts in the Text**
Inferences about connection to concept:	Text support or prior knowledge support:
Inferences about connection to concept:	Text support or prior knowledge support:

Insightful Interpretations

Directions: Use this graphic organizer to read for significant information and to gather insightful interpretations from yourself, a partner, and your teacher.

Text Information	My Interpretation
My Partner's Interpretations	**My Teacher's Interpretations**

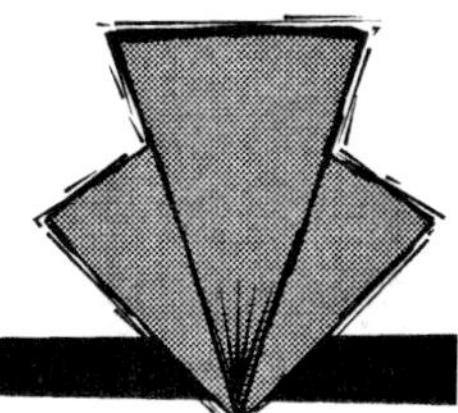

Partnered Reading

Directions: In the top boxes, each partner should record significant text information. Then each should use the thinking stems below to make an inference about the text.

This information connects to. . .
I think that. . .
I visualize. . .
I predict. . .
Perhaps the author wants us to think that. . .

Partner #1: Significant Text Information	Partner #2: Significant Text Information
Partner #1: Inference About the Text	**Partner #2: Inference About the Text**

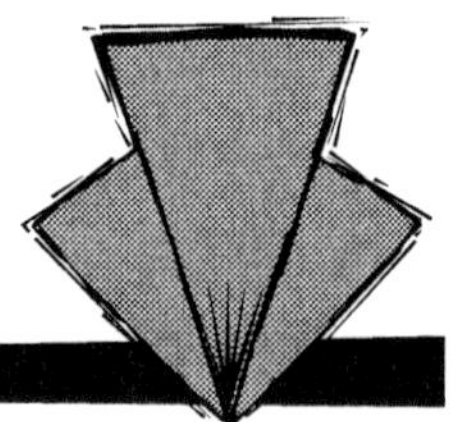

Perceptive Predictions

Directions: Make a prediction about the information.

Issue or Problem:

Proposed Solution:

Pros	Cons

Prediction: What are the author's beliefs about the topic? What does the author expect you to do with the information you have gained?

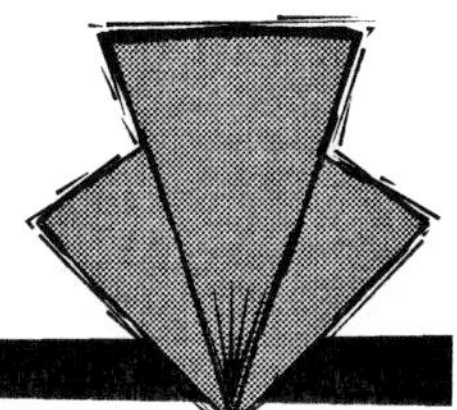

Text Feature Inferencing

Directions: Make inferences about the text features.

Concept being studied: ______________________________

Guiding questions: ______________________________

____

Text Feature (charts, graphs, diagrams, pictures, illustrations, captions, photographs)	**Inference about the text feature's connection to the major concept**

Artistic Inferencing

Directions: Recognize the inferencing that goes on in your mind with a drawing.

Words or phrases from the text describing the topic or concept: ______________________________

____

____

____

Illustration of Idea or Concept

Look back at your illustration. What information (details, ideas, colors, etc.) did you include in the illustration that were not described in the text?

____

____

____

Why did you add the information that you did to your illustration?

____

____

____

Setting the Purpose

Setting the Purpose

Introduction

All meaningful reading needs a purpose. Even without explicitly or consciously stating why they are reading, strategic readers survey the reading material and assess why they are reading it. This technique helps to establish how to read a particular piece of writing. The traditional setting for teachers to provide students with a purpose for reading is when giving an assignment. Although helpful to some students, this method does not allow students to determine their own purposes for reading. Consequently, less proficient readers wait until the purpose is set for them and then read only to obtain that small piece of specified information. Very little actual learning takes place in this setting.

The process of reading should begin before a book is opened. Teachers can help students become effective, systematic readers by teaching strategies that reinforce the purpose for reading a piece of nonfiction text.

Stating the Purpose for Reading

Most of the time we give students their purpose for reading. We tell them that they will be reading to learn about a particular topic, such as the Civil War in social studies, the French Impressionists in art, or habitats for various animals in science. Secondary school students must be able to identify their own purposes for reading as well as reading for an assigned purpose. Expose students to the idea that people read for different purposes that include reading in order to:

- be entertained, informed, or persuaded.
- learn how to do something.
- analyze the author.
- reflect upon and extend personal experience and prior knowledge.
- generate questions for further research about the topic or concept.
- gather information for a discussion.

It is important that students keep their purpose in mind while reading so that they can sort and organize the new information, connect it to their purpose for reading, and articulate and justify how the information they have gained helps them achieve their purpose for reading.

Choosing Appropriate Materials to Read

Once students know and understand their purpose for reading, they should be given opportunities to select texts that will help them to achieve their purpose. Students need to be taught how to preview the text, skim for main ideas and supporting details, make note of headings and subheadings, critically analyze graphic features, and carefully read the back cover, inside cover, and any other surface information that will help them to determine the appropriateness of the text.

Setting the Purpose

Using Appropriate Strategies for Different Purposes

Being able to set the purpose for reading is a vital first step toward developing strategic reading skills. Students need to be able to skim and scan effectively to locate information quickly. They need to be able to read carefully in order to gain full comprehension and read critically in order to analyze or interpret the author's intent. These are just some of the skills that students need to acquire in order to meet the purpose for reading. Make sure to expose students to text coding, double-entry journals, partner journals, discussion techniques, and graphic organizers in order for them to read for entertainment, information, critical analysis of the author, or whatever their purpose may be.

Enjoying Nonfiction Text

Reading nonfiction opens a world of opportunities for learning about many diverse and interesting topics. Having students conduct I-Search projects in which they identify a topic of interest to them, brainstorm questions related to the topic and then conduct research can expose them to a wealth of nonfiction reading. Make sure to teach students to analyze text features including charts, graphs, diagrams, and maps and their relationship to the author's purpose.

Solving Problems

One of the most compelling purposes for reading is to solve a problem. Have students generate topics of interest and problems that concern them. These problems can be related to local, state, national, or international issues. Have students read from a multitude of nonfiction sources in order to solve the problem or at least to gain information to understand the issue more completely.

Forming an Opinion

Another purpose for reading that is highly motivating for students is reading to form an opinion. Secondary school students have their own ideas about many topics. Teachers need to coach students in researching different viewpoints to form an intelligent opinion, one that they can back up with statistics, details, and more specific information.

Skimming for Facts

When students have identified a motivating and focused purpose for reading, model how to skim for facts. Skimming involves reading chapter headings and subheadings, the chapter introductions and summaries, and the questions, if any, at the end of a chapter. Next, read any information that is given special attention by different typeface, different color print, plus graphics and their captions. Students must be able to read to gain information from a multitude of sources. To tackle as many sources as possible, students will need to skim information quickly, discern which information matches their purpose for reading, and decide which information needs careful study.

Setting the Purpose

Discovering Models

As students are reading, make sure to emphasize that they are also writers. Students must understand that when they read and think about how the author is affecting them, they will better understand how to affect the readers of their writing. Teach them to be critical readers who are able to identify organizational patterns in text, text features, key vocabulary, and rhetorical techniques.

Establishing and Adjusting Purposes

When students conduct their own research, give them guidance in selecting a topic of interest to them. Then ask them to formulate a research question that, in essence, will establish their purpose for reading. As they read and do research, have students adjust their purpose for reading by refining and revising their initial research question. Inform them that professional researchers follow the same process. By establishing and adjusting purposes for reading, students will learn how to be strategic thinkers and problem solvers while reading.

Using Characteristics to Choose Nonfiction Material

Often teachers will present students with characteristics for selecting their nonfiction reading material. As an alternative, in order to build independence in students, allow them to generate their own characteristics or criteria for choosing nonfiction material. Examples may include criteria that the material connects to a specific topic, contains text features, has multiple viewpoints, and is highly engaging in physical appearance and presentation. Have students discuss these characteristics and evaluate whether or not the nonfiction material that they have selected has these characteristics.

Using Strategies Independently

Model how students should set their own purposes for reading. Start at the school library and allow them to browse through books at least once every three weeks and to select a book for enjoyment. Once students have selected books, have them share with the class what they chose and why. Allow them to choose fiction and nonfiction. Expose students to a variety of techniques for book selection: examining the book jacket and the inside cover, reading about the author, scanning the chapter titles, reading the first few paragraphs, etc. Make book selection a celebration of independent choice.

Setting the Purpose

Strategy 1: Evaluating Purpose

Allow students to select books of their choice and have them identify many purposes for reading those books. Have students complete the graphic organizer, Evaluating Purpose (page 212), by recording their purposes, by identifying whether or not they achieved their purposes, and by writing a brief explanation that evaluates why they did or did not achieve their purpose. Have students compare their evaluations with a partner.

Strategy 2: Text Coding

A simple coding strategy that will help students read to achieve their purpose is identified on the Text Coding for Purpose worksheet (page 213). As students are reading, have them mark the text a "P!" for a strong connection to purpose and a "P" for some connection to purpose. (If students are not allowed to write directly in the text, have them use sticky notes.) When they finish reading the nonfiction text, have them record the text information that corresponds with the code that they chose in the left column of the chart and then write a reaction to the selected text in the right column. Have students reflect on how the information connects to their purpose for reading and their prior knowledge of the subject.

Strategy 3: Question/Answer

Begin by having students identify their purpose for reading. Then lead them in generating a list of pre-reading questions that will help them to achieve their purpose. For example, if students are reading about the history of baseball and their purpose is to understand the history and know why it's important to the sport today, they may generate several questions, such as 1) Who invented the game of baseball? 2) Where was it invented? 3) What were the initial reactions to the game? 4) How do people react to the game today? Students should write their questions in the left column of the Question/Answer chart (page 214) and record the answers as they find them in the text in the right column. Remind students that to answer some of the questions they may need to make inferences. When they have finished their charts, have them reflect on how the process of questioning helped them to achieve their purpose for reading.

Strategy 4: Question/Answer/Opinion

Follow the same procedures as the Question/Answer strategy. However, this time have students write brief opinions about the topics they researched. Some helpful sentence starters include:

- I was surprised to learn that . . .
- This information confirms what I knew about. . .
- I agree/disagree because. . .

Use the Question/Answer/Opinion worksheet on page 215 for this activity.

Setting the Purpose

Strategy 5: Examining Multiple Texts

A great way to motivate students to examine multiple texts is to present them with a purpose for reading; then take them to the school library to select books to achieve their purpose. For example, imagine that the students' purpose for reading is to learn about the solar system. Have them use the Examining Multiple Texts worksheet (page 216) to preview three different texts and to think about how the text would help them to achieve their purpose for reading. Instruct students to select the best text and to read more deeply to acquire the necessary information.

Strategy 6: Author and Me Analysis

It is important for students to understand that they read for a variety of purposes, but authors also write for a variety of purposes. Use the Author and Me Analysis worksheet (page 217) to have students identify their purpose and the author's purpose. Chances are that if the student is reading to be informed, the author was also writing for the student's information. As students are reading, have them record important information in the left column and make connections to their purpose for reading and the author's purpose for writing in the remaining columns. Another worksheet for this strategy is on page 218.

Strategy 7: Purpose and Solving Problems

One of the most important things for educators to do is to teach students that they can read in order to solve problems and important issues. It is vital for students to know that text contains information that is highly interesting and motivating. Expose students to interesting, engaging text as often as possible. Have them use the Purpose and Solving Problems worksheet (page 219) to record problems and issues that they encounter in their reading in the left column and then think about whether they better understand the issue and how they will act upon it in the right column. To create an educational atmosphere that sends the message that reading is fun, make sure to have many nonfiction materials available to students.

Strategy 8: Reading and Skimming for Facts

In content-area classrooms, one of the most common purposes for reading is to be informed. Create an atmosphere where learning is valuable and informational text is viewed as intriguing. Distribute the Reading and Skimming for Facts worksheet (page 220) and have the students record facts and details in the left column and write a reaction in the right column. Make sure students think about why the author wanted them to learn the information, why the information will be valuable to them, and any further questions they may have.

Setting the Purpose

Strategy 9: Reading to be Persuaded

We are surrounded by text that is intended to be persuasive. Have students read a variety of texts that are persuasive and show them how to analyze the author's use of rhetorical language, examples, and appeals to the audience to make his or her argument convincing. Distribute the Purpose and Being Persuaded worksheet (page 221) and have students record text information that is persuasive. In the right column, have them write a reaction in which they think about the choices that the author made and why those choices made the text convincing. Allow students to identify ideas with which they disagree or text that is not convincing.

Strategy 10: Reading to Extend Prior Knowledge

Extending and enriching students' prior knowledge about a subject can be very beneficial in deepening their understanding. As an introductory activity to reading information on a topic that is already familiar to students, have them sit in a circle. In round-robin fashion ask them to share something they know about the topic or concept. As a variation, begin with a K-W-L chart to help them identify their prior knowledge. Distribute the Purpose and Extending Prior Knowledge worksheet (page 222) and have students record in the left column information that connects to what they already know as they are reading. In the right column, have them write a reaction in which they connect to their personal experience and/or prior knowledge. Encourage students to write about information that surprised them or confirmed what they already knew.

Strategy 11: Reading and Following Directions

Students will encounter sets of instructions, recipes, and rule books their entire lives and need to know how to read critically in order to create a product or learn how to do something. Have students identify something that they would like to learn how to do or to make. Take them to the school library and allow them to find resources that fit their learning objectives. Distribute the Purpose and Following Directions worksheet (page 223), and have them record the step-by-step instructions in the left column in paraphrased form. Have them write a reaction by analyzing whether the instructions were clear, determining the effectiveness of the graphic features, and identifying any further questions they have based on areas of confusion.

Setting the Purpose

Strategy 12: Partnered Reading

Have students read for a common purpose and gather text information to achieve their purpose on the Partnered Reading worksheet (page 224). Then have them discuss the text they read and write a reaction about how the information connects to what they already know and whether or not they have any further questions.

Strategy 13: Skimming for Purpose

Skimming focuses on the general information and is an important skill to utilize when students are learning to take effective notes. Skimming involves reading chapter headings and subheadings, the chapter introductions and summaries, and the questions, if any, at the end of a chapter. Next, read any information that is given special attention by different typeface, different print color, plus graphics and their captions.

Strategy 14: Selective Reading Guide

Prepare a Selective Reading Guide (Cunningham & Shablak, 1975) to teach students to use their textbooks as a resource rather than as a book to be read from cover to cover. This strategy is particularly effective with struggling or reluctant readers because it notifies them about which information is most essential and helps them to see how to establish a purpose for reading. Here is an example:

page 186

Paragraphs 1 & 2—Introduce the section. Read them quickly.

Paragraphs 3 & 4—Define an ocean and its importance to our planet. Know the names of the world's oceans and their locations on a world map or globe.

page 187

Paragraph 1—Based on the information in this paragraph, make a list of the world's five oceans in order of their size.

Paragraphs 2 & 3—Pay attention to differences in the oceans' average temperatures and their effect on the world's weather.

Paragraphs 4 & 5—Skim these paragraphs.

Evaluating Purpose

Directions: Identify your purposes for reading. Be very specific. For example, if your purpose is to be informed, identify specifically the information about which you would like to be informed. After reading, determine whether you achieved your purpose and write an explanation.

What are my purposes for reading?	**Did I achieve my purpose?**	**Explanation**
	YES NO	
	YES NO	
	YES NO	
	YES NO	
	YES NO	
	YES NO	

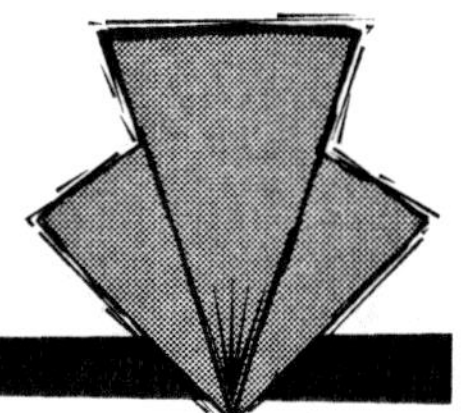

Text Coding for Purpose

Directions: Before reading, identify your purpose. As you are reading, mark in the text or on a sticky note using the codes. Then record the text that corresponds with the codes in the left column. Write a reaction using the guiding questions in the right column.

P! = Strong Connection to Purpose for Reading
P = Some Connection to Purpose for Reading

Purpose for Reading: ____

____

Text Information that Connects to Your Purpose for Reading	**Reaction:** How does this information connect to your purpose for reading? How does this information connect to your prior knowledge of the subject? What further questions do you have?

Question/Answer

Directions: Before reading, record questions that will help you to achieve your purpose for reading. As you read, record the answers to the questions.

My purpose for reading: ______________________________

My Questions About the Text Information	Answers

How did questioning help me to achieve my purpose for reading?

____

____

____

____

Question/Answer/Opinion

Directions: Before reading, use this chart to record questions that will help you to achieve your purpose for reading. Record the answers as you read. After reading, write an opinion about the text information you found.

My purpose for reading: ____

____

My Questions	Answers	My Opinions

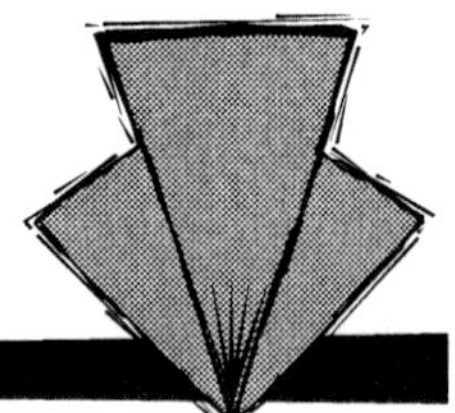

Examining Multiple Texts

Directions: Look through three different texts. Establish your purpose for reading. Compare each text and determine how each text will help you achieve your purpose for reading.

Purpose for Reading: ______________________________

____

Text #1: ______________________________

Information gained through previewing (topics, concepts, ideas): ______________________________

____

____

____

How will this text help me to achieve my purpose for reading? ______________________________

____

____

____

Text #2: ______________________________

Information gained through previewing (topics, concepts, ideas): ______________________________

____

____

____

How will this text help me to achieve my purpose for reading? ______________________________

____

____

____

Text #3: ______________________________

Information gained through previewing (topics, concepts, ideas): ______________________________

____

____

____

How will this text help me to achieve my purpose for reading? ______________________________

____

____

Author and Me Analysis

Directions: Compare your purpose for reading with the author's purpose for writing.

My purpose for reading: ____

____

The author's purpose for writing: ____

____

Important Information	How does this information connect to the author's purpose?	How does this information connect to my purpose for reading?

Purpose and Analyzing the Author

Directions: Your purpose for reading is to analyze the author. As you read, record text information that reveals the author's purpose on the left side of the chart and then react to the information on the right side of the chart.

Title of the text: ______________________________

Text information that reveals the author's purpose	**Reaction:** What does the author want me to learn about the topic? What language choices does the author use to achieve his or her purpose? What graphic features does the author include to achieve his or her purpose? How do the author's examples achieve his or her purpose?

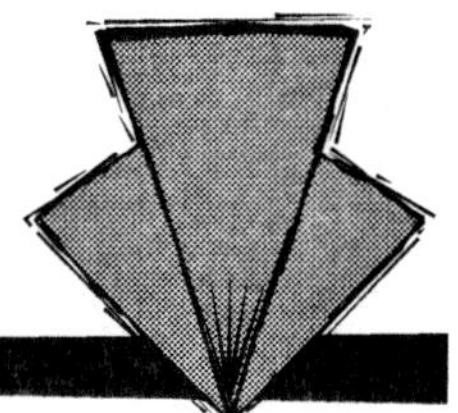

Purpose and Solving Problems

Directions: Your purpose for reading is to solve a problem. As you read, record text information that helps you identify the problem on the left side of the chart and then react to the information on the right side of the chart.

Research Question: ____

____

Text that helps me to identify the problem	**Reaction:** How does the text make me feel? How does the information help me to better understand the problem? What further problems or issues can I think of after reading?

Setting the Purpose

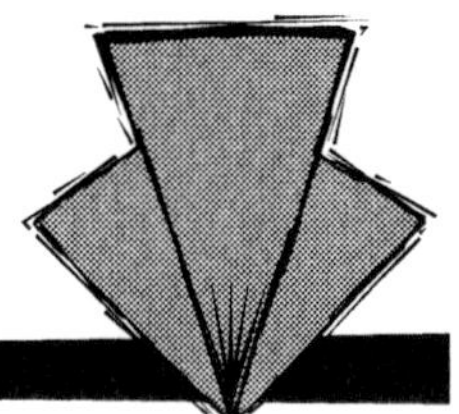

Reading and Skimming for Facts

Directions: Your purpose for reading is to skim for facts and determine which facts are important. As you read, record text information that is informative, factual, or helps you to learn about the topic or concept. Record text information that is informative on the left side of the chart and then react to the information on the right side of the chart.

Title of the text: ____

____

____

Text information that helps you learn about the topic or concept	**Reaction:** What was the most important information you learned? What were the most important facts or details you learned? Why? What did the author want you to learn from this information? Do you have any further questions?

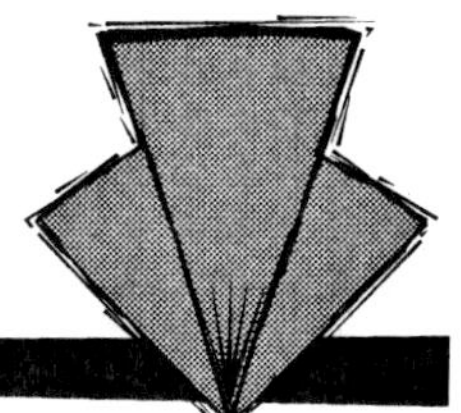

Purpose and Being Persuaded

Directions: Your purpose for reading is to be persuaded about the topic. As you read, record text information that is convincing and persuasive on the left side of the chart and then react to the information on the right side of the chart.

Title of the text: ____

Text information that is convincing or persuasive (Remember to examine carefully the content of the text and the graphic features.)	**Reaction:** Why is this information persuasive? Does the author use language, examples, or graphic features that are particularly convincing? Explain. Will you take action as a result of this information? How could the information be more persuasive?

Is there any part of the text that you don't agree with or that is not convincing? Explain.

____

____

____

Purpose and Extending Prior Knowledge

Directions: Your purpose for reading is to extend your prior knowledge. As you read, record text information that connects to what you already know about the topic or concept on the left side of the chart and then react to the information on the right side of the chart.

Title of the text: ______________________________

Text information that connects to your personal experience or prior knowledge of the topic or concept	**Reaction:** How does this information connect to your personal experience or prior knowledge? Does this information surprise you or confirm what you already know? Do you agree or disagree with any of the information? Explain.

Purpose and Following Directions

Directions: Your purpose for reading is to follow directions. As you read, record text information that teaches you how to achieve your task on the left side of the chart and then react to the information on the right side of the chart.

Title of the text: ______________________________

Text information that shows the step-by-step nature of the directions	**Reaction:** Are the instructions clear? How could the instructions be clearer? How could the author have included more graphic features to clarify the instructions? What questions do you still have? Based on what you learned, could you teach someone else how to achieve the task?

Partnered Reading

Directions: Both you and your buddy have the same purpose for reading. Gather information to achieve your purpose and then react to the information.

Purpose for reading: ______________________________

Partner #1: Text information that helps to achieve the purpose for reading:	**Partner #2:** Text information that helps to achieve the purpose for reading:
Partner #1: Reaction (How does this information connect to what you already know about the topic? What further questions do you have?)	**Partner #2:** Reaction (How does this information connect to what you already know about the topic? What further questions do you have?)

Questioning

Questioning

Introduction

What is the difference between active and passive readers? Active, skilled readers approach nonfiction text with such questions as "What is the meaning of the title?", "What type of text is this?", and "What does the author mean by this statement?" Finally, they think beyond the text with more questions after they have finished reading, for example, "Where can I find additional facts?" Their active questioning leads them to the next piece of text, the next piece of information. Through questioning, learning becomes an on-going process.

Passive readers, on the other hand, may not realize that their comprehension might be improved by forming their own questions as they read. Passive readers miss making rich connections within the text and between their personal experience and the text when they do not ask questions. Each reading assignment becomes a dead end rather than an invitation.

To turn passive readers into active ones, teachers need to model not only the process of questioning, but also an enthusiastic embrace of the process. Teachers must also model different types of questions. There are questions that require a simple factual answer, questions that require critical thinking, and even questions that perhaps never will be answered, such as "Why does every living thing eventually die?"

In addition to modeling, teachers must give students skills to generate questions on their own. Some methods, such as brainstorming, are freewheeling ways for students to form questions. Others, such as journalistic questions, give students a systematic method for creating useful questions.

Good questions engage a student's curiosity, encourage original thinking, assess a student's ability to recall and infer, and even prompt additional questions. Good questions excite and motivate reading. They propose and predict ideas. They help readers check for understanding. They beg for answers and are not easily brushed aside.

How is reading proficiency developed through reading? Questions are particularly motivating to secondary school students because they are at a point in their lives where they want to understand and make sense of the world. When students are reading, questioning strategies can help arouse curiosity, provide direction for research, formulate a purpose for reading, and stimulate further reading and investigation about a topic.

In an educational climate driven by assessment and accountability, it is important to understand the difference between assessment questions and genuine learning questions. Typical assessment questions are those questions that we already know the answer to and that we use to measure the academic achievement of students. Genuine learning questions are those questions to which we do not know the answers, that arouse our curiosity, and that require further inquiry on the part of both the teacher and the student. There is a place in the classroom for both kinds of questions, and it is essential that students become proficient at using reading strategies that allow them to answer both kinds of questions accurately, elaborately, and confidently.

Questioning

Categorizing and Differentiating Among Questions

When students are able to categorize the kinds of questions they are being asked, they are better able to understand their purpose for reading. Understanding and applying such strategies as the Question/Answer Relationships strategy can aid readers in knowing the kinds of reading and thinking they have to do in order to answer a question. In addition, question coding can help readers categorize a variety of different kinds of questions they will encounter across content areas. The skill of categorizing is one that is useful both in school and various real-world contexts.

Monitoring Comprehension

When teachers model reading strategies, it is important that they know how to release the responsibility gradually to students. Students must have access to a variety of strategies in order to clarify, revise, and reformulate their initial understandings of text content. There are two types of explicit modeling (Roehler and Duffy, 1991) that can ensure that students move toward taking responsibility for monitoring their reading comprehension: *talk alouds* and *think alouds*. In a *talk aloud*, the teacher presents students with the components of a monitoring strategy and then orally leads them through these steps by showing students how to apply the strategy. It is useful to make an overhead transparency of the steps of the strategy. For instance, when a graphic organizer is being introduced to the class, the teacher tells students the steps necessary to fill in the different parts of the organizer, but doesn't fill them in. Usually, in an introductory lesson, the teacher would show students the exact procedures needed to fill in the graphic organizer and do a sample in front of the class. The following is a partial example of a talk aloud for a web organizer:

Teacher: I've written the steps that you should follow to fill in a web.

Step 1: Read the selection to determine the main idea. Write it in the center oval.

Step 2: Reread the selection. This time stop as you identify details that support the main idea.

Step 3: Write each supporting detail in the boxes surrounding the main idea.

Step 4: Make sure all the boxes for supporting details are filled in.

Step 5: Use the information on your web to write a summary of the selection you just read.

The teacher then takes students through the process necessary to do the steps but doesn't model aloud the thinking done to find the main idea or details, write the main idea or details, or write the summary. In Step 5 the teacher might say, "When you have finished your web, you will use all the information to write a summary of what you read." Then students apply the strategy to a text. Teachers use talk alouds to teach students how to use strategies.

Questioning

Monitoring Comprehension *(cont.)*

Think alouds (Clark, 1984; Meichenbaum, 1985) require the teacher to present the steps of the strategy and then share the actual thinking that accompanies the use of this strategy. Teachers should make their own confusion, misconceptions, general wonderings, and discoveries apparent. It is important to show students that an adult reader also has to wonder, clarify, and question in order to understand text information and that an adult can experience delight when finding the answer.

Organizing Content Knowledge

Students need to have a variety of techniques for acquiring content knowledge. In order to help them, teachers should consider focusing instruction on key concepts. The following are some basic questions that you can ask yourself when planning a unit:

1. What is the major concept being investigated or studied?
2. What are the guiding questions that will help students make sense of this topic?
3. What texts will I use to help students find answers to the guiding questions?
4. How will I help students organize the information that they find in order to maximize their content knowledge and its connections to the major concept?

The Reading Process

To become proficient readers, students must understand that reading is a process and that there are specific behaviors to engage in before, during, and after reading. Questioning skills must be developed at each stage of the reading process, and these questions can focus on either the content of the text or the process of reading. The following questions can be shared with students to guide their thinking before, during, and after reading:

Before

What do I already know about the topic?

How do the title, headings, and subheadings reveal information about the topic?

What strategies do I know that could help me make sense of the text?

During

What new information am I learning in order to clarify my original understanding of the topic?

What strategies can I use to monitor my comprehension of the major themes and concepts?

After

What is my overall understanding of the topic?

What strategy was most effective in making sense of the information?

Questioning

Accessing Prior Knowledge

Students must access their prior knowledge in order to construct meaning. The following is a step-by-step process for connecting prior knowledge to the content learned during daily instruction. Post these questions on a chart or on the board to help guide students throughout their learning experiences in your classroom.

- What do I already know about the topic?
- How does the text connect to what I know?
- How does the connection further my understanding of the topic?

Inferencing

Students will need to be adept at inferencing in order to make sense of complex text. Well-developed inferencing skills allow them to connect their prior knowledge to the text and to comprehend the information at much deeper levels. The following are some questions that students can ask themselves to build inferencing skills:

- How do I interpret this information?
- What are my observations after looking at headings, subheadings, and pictures?
- How does my prior knowledge help me to make reasonable inferences?

Asking Questions to Seek Elaboration and Clarification

Students must be able to clarify and elaborate upon their initial understandings of text. In order to access deeper levels of meaning in the text, it is important for students to be able to ask themselves questions, such as:

1. What is the information teaching me about the topic?
2. What is the author's message?
3. How do the details enrich my understanding of the main concept?

Questioning

Strategy Instruction

The following strategies will help build students' proficiencies as readers. Adapt these strategies to suit the needs of your classroom. Remember the gradual release of responsibility. It is essential that students learn to use these strategies independently. This independence is achieved through teacher modeling, direct instruction, talk alouds, think alouds, and the expectation that students will internalize the modeling and apply the strategies to their own reading.

Strategy 1: Trivial Pursuit and Brain Quest

Divide students into teams and ask general questions from such games as Trivial Pursuit and Brain Quest. Give students a day to research various topics of interest and generate their own questions that can be used for cooperative games to answer knowledge-based questions. Gradually incorporate questions from concepts that students are learning in your classroom and require students to make inferences and extend their thinking.

Strategy 2: Partners-Question

Students write five questions on a slip of paper using their class notes and information from the text. Pair students with a partner, and each partner asks a question while the other partner answers. This strategy helps students review material before a quiz, develop listening skills, and check for understanding during a lesson or unit.

Strategy 3: Question Webs

Question Web (page 237) is a great way for students to gather information about one question. These questions can be student- or teacher-generated. Students record their question in the center of the web. Then they read and research the answers to the question by accessing a variety of resources. It is particularly motivating to students if they can work as a team to gather the information to answer the question at the center of the web. After gathering enough information, they work together to synthesize what they have learned into a coherent response. Students will need you to model the synthesis of information gained. Have a sample Question Web on large butcher paper and then use two highlighters to code essential and extraneous information. Demonstrate how to blend, combine, and connect the essential information into a response to the question.

Strategy 4: Discussion Questions

Students often say they do not know what types of questions to ask when having a discussion about a text. Provide students with the list of discussion questions on page 238 to use to facilitate class or small-group discussions. Students can also use this list independently to guide their thinking while they read.

Questioning

Strategy 5: Question/Answer Relationships (QAR)

Teaching students to understand question/answer relationships can greatly aid their abilities to answer questions proficiently. QAR is a strategy to teach students how to find answers to questions, especially those for which the answer may not be found in the actual text. Raphael (1982), who developed this technique, identified three types of questions:

Right-there questions: Questions for which answers are easily found in the text.

Think-and-search questions: Questions for which answers are in the text but are embedded within the text in a way that makes them more difficult to find. Whereas right-there questions might simply be inverted into statements to suggest the answer, think-and-search questions might be worded quite differently from the statements which answer them.

On-your-own questions: Questions for which the answers are not in the text. Students will need to think about the answer (On My Own) or go to another resource besides the text itself (Author and Me).

Example

This strategy used in social studies might elicit the following questions for the subject of Egyptian religion:

1. Right-there question: Who was the god of the living and the dead?
2. Think-and-search question: What beliefs did people have about Amon-Re?
3. On-my-own question: Why would religion be important to the people?
4. Author-and-me question: Why would Egyptians prepare so much for the afterlife?

This strategy used in math on the topic of an integer might look like the following:

1. Right-there question: What is an integer?
2. Think-and-search question: What types of integers are there?
3. On-my-own question: When would I use negative numbers?
4. Author-and-me question: How would I balance a checkbook?

Use the activity sheet on page 239 to guide students through the identification of questions. Then, have students read a particular piece of text and use the appropriate code to apply their knowledge of QAR.

Questioning

Strategy 6: Stance Questioning

Stance questioning is a way to gain a picture of where the reader "stands" in relation to the text. When readers "enter" into text, they begin to form a global understanding of the text. As they "move" through the text, they develop their interpretations and further their initial understandings. As they "exit" the text, they are able to relate personal experiences and prior knowledge to the text information. When readers have fully exited the text and gained some distance, they are able to analyze the author's decisions (based on the work of Judith Langer, 1987). Stance questions can be divided into four categories:

Global Understanding—Being Out and Stepping Into the Text

Developing an Interpretation—Being In and Moving Through the Text

Reflecting on Personal Experiences—Being In and Stepping Out of the Text

Critical Response—Stepping Out and Analyzing the Reading Experience

Use the activity sheet on page 240 to allow students to choose questions within these categories to guide them as they move through the reading process.

Strategy 7: Double-Entry Journals

When students use double-entry journals, they are able to see the connection between the text and their thinking. Instruct students to divide their notebook paper in half and record text information on the left side and their reflections, questions, and/or responses on the right side. This strategic tool teaches students that they are not merely reading words and that their brains should be actively making note of both the text and the thinking that goes on in relation to the text. Have students read content-related text and use the double-entry journal (page 241) to exercise their metacognitive skills.

Strategy 8: Digging Deeper

Students will begin by listing random, unconnected questions about a given topic. But as their reading and questioning skills improve, encourage them to build their questions so that each answer creates a deeper understanding of the topic or concept under investigation. Have students use the Digging Deeper chart (page 242) during or after reading to record significant text information and reflect on that text information by responding to the sentence starters on the right side of the chart.

Questioning

Strategy 9: Coding for Quality Questioning

Coding text is useful during reading to ensure that students engage with the information as they are reading. You can create codes simply by thinking of the topics, concepts, or ideas that you want students to reflect upon and then assigning a single letter to represent that idea. A particularly powerful set of codes includes the following: text-to-self (T-S), text-to-text (T-T); and text-to-world (T-W). Readers will consciously make note of times when the text connects to their own lives, to another text, and to information related to the world. Students can write the codes directly on the text or on sticky notes. Use the reproducible on page 243 to have students use the codes to make more detailed reflections on the text.

Strategy 10: Text Questioning

Have students preview the text and generate as many questions as possible on the board. Then read the text aloud with students pausing during reading to record more questions on the class list. After reading, record any final questions. Then go through the list and discuss the questions, placing a code of "T" next to any questions that were answered explicitly in the text. Discuss the remaining questions and how conceptual knowledge or inferences are needed to answer these questions.

Strategy 11: Concept and Fact Questions

Provide students with two sizes of sticky notes—large and small—to use when finding a concept or a fact. Instruct them to read the text information and record questions that require inferencing, reference to concept knowledge, connections to other texts or information learned, or further research on the large sticky notes. Essentially students are capturing the big ideas on the concept sticky notes. Instruct the students to record fact-based questions, right-there questions, and questions about vocabulary on the little sticky notes, intended to represent smaller ideas. After reading, create a T-chart on the board, labeled "Concept Questions" on the left side and "Fact Questions" on the right side. Students place their sticky notes in the appropriate column. Discuss whether the questions are "correct" in that they do represent conceptual or factual information. Allow students to come to the board to choose a sticky note to which they will respond either orally or in writing. A template for a T-chart can be found on page 244 for students to use independently with other texts.

Questioning

Strategy 12: Question Squares

As students read, they should ask questions about what they are reading. Sometimes these questions can be asked of oneself, the author, the teacher, or other classmates. Using the chart on page 245, students can record key information from their reading and then think of questions for these different audiences.

Strategy 13: Questions Before, During, and After

Using the chart on page 246, students can write the many questions they have before, during, and after reading. They can also record speculations and predictions. Having a chart to record this information provides some structure to help students guide their thinking. After reading, they can think of questions they still have and also record possible answers. This activity works well in small groups or pairs or with a student working independently.

Strategy 14: Questions on Trial

Use this strategy once students understand the importance of asking questions before, during, and after reading. Create a panel of four student judges who will analyze their classmates' questions. The panel must explain why a question is "good" or "better" based on the question's ability to enhance the knowledge of the questioner. There are no "bad" questions, only good questions and better questions. Assign weaker students to be judges only after they have seen several different panels of student judges. Here is an example of one panel's assessment of classmates' questions:

Good question: When did Christopher Columbus discover America?

Panel's analysis: This is a good question, but it is very narrow. All you will learn from it is a date.

Better question: Why did Christopher Columbus set sail across the Atlantic Ocean?

Panel's analysis: This is a better question. It will lead you to a major understanding.

Good question: How was Christopher Columbus received by the natives he met?

Panel's analysis: This is a good question, especially if you give an explanation rather than a one-word answer.

Better question: What were the consequences of Christopher Columbus's discovery of America?

Panel's analysis: This is a better question because it will help you to find out what happened in the long run.

Questioning

Strategy 15: Question Exchange

A question exchange lets students review information using their own questions. Each student prepares five thought-provoking questions and answers; these questions cannot have "yes" or "no" answers. Each student poses one of these questions to a classmate in round-robin fashion. The classmate gives an answer. If that answer is correct, then he or she asks a question of the next student. If the answer is wrong, then the one who asked the question asks the next student until a correct answer is given. It is best if students ask a question that has not already been asked; however, if necessary, they may repeat one. This strategy is good for review before a test because each student knows the answers to his or her original five questions plus the answers to all questions presented in class. The following is a sample of this strategy in action:

Alicia: (to Benito) "What territories did the U.S. acquire as a result of the Spanish-American War?"

Benito: "Puerto Rico, the Philippines, and Guam."

Alicia: "Right."

Benito: (to Christa) "When did the Spanish-American War begin and when did it end?"

Christa: "1861 to 1865."

Benito: "Sorry, that's wrong."

Benito: (to Dylan) "When did the Spanish-American War begin and when did it end?"

Dylan: "The Spanish-American War started and ended in 1898."

Benito: "Correct."

Strategy 16: What if. . . poems

After you have presented a topic or concept to students, have them work in groups to write a "What if. . . poem." Instruct students to record all of their questions about the topic by starting with the sentence starter "What if. . . ." Post the poems around the classroom and have students refer to them throughout learning the new topic or concept. Following is a sample of a poem with questions about bats:

- I wonder how a bat got its name.
- I wonder what bats like to eat.
- I wonder if bats are a kind of bird.
- I wonder where a bat lives.
- I wonder if bats are a friend or foe of humans.

Question Web

Directions: Write your question in the center circle. As you read, listen, or do research, record your answers on the outer spokes of the web.

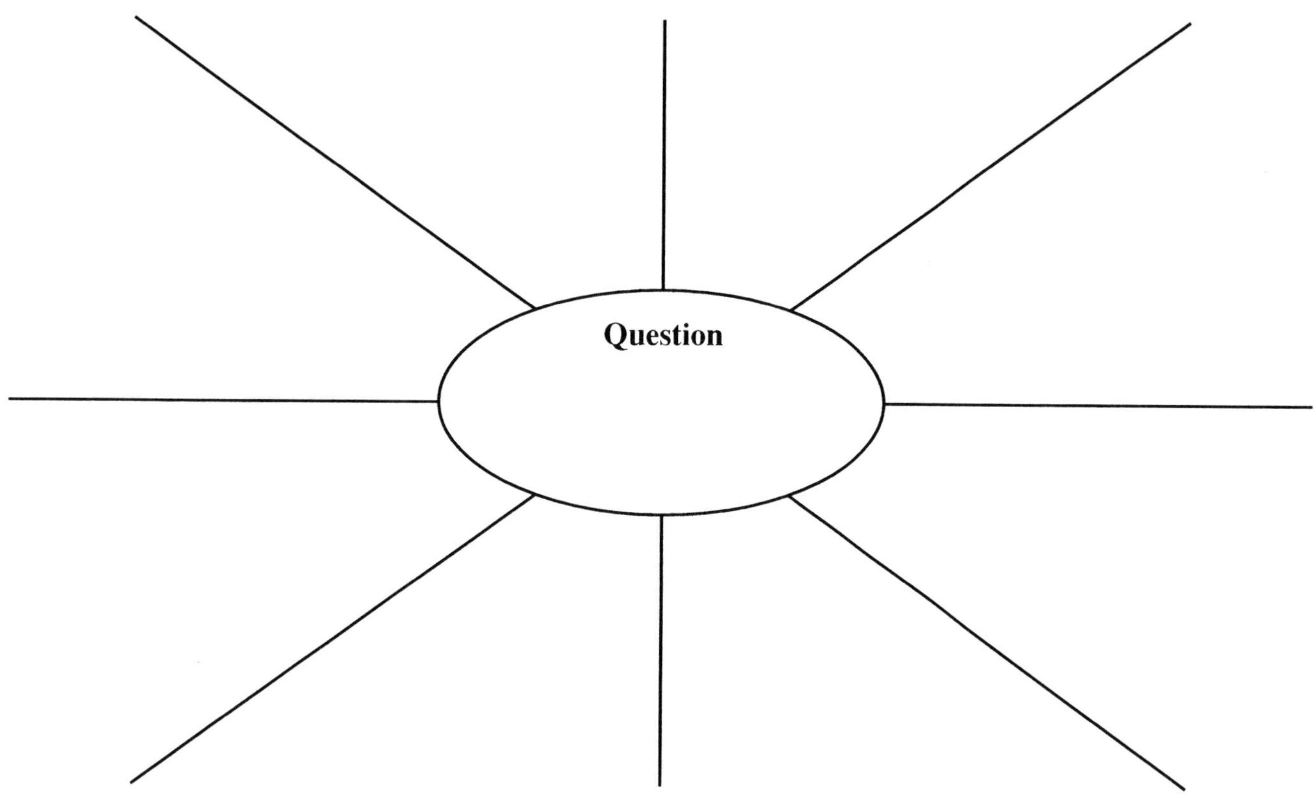

Synthesis of information: Use the most important text information to write a response to the question in the center of your web.

Questions for Discussion

Questions for thinking about text content:

- What is the main idea of the text?
- What are the "big ideas" in the text?
- What is most interesting?
- What did you find confusing?
- Did you learn anything new?
- Did you learn anything that surprised or concerned you?

Questions for thinking about world connections:

- What do you already know about this topic?
- How does the text connect to topics or concepts you are learning in class?
- What new questions do you have about this topic?
- What current events connect to this topic?

Questions for thinking about a strategic approach:

- What parts of the text are difficult or confusing?
- What parts of the text are boring?
- What strategies can you use to make the text interesting?
- What strategies can you use to better understand the text?
- Did your strategic attempts work? Explain.
- What new strategies can you use?
- Can you use part of a strategy you have learned to help you?
- Do you need to create a new strategy?
- What are your overall beliefs about the text and how did you form these beliefs?

Questions for understanding the process of reading:

- What new information did you learn about reading?
- How can you apply your knowledge to reading other texts?
- Why is a strategic approach to reading important?
- What advice can you give to other readers about the process of reading?

Question/Answer Relationships

Part A Directions: Read the following information aloud. Observe the differences among each of these four kinds of questions.

In the Text	In My Head
Right There: The answer to the question can be found easily and immediately in the text. The words used to create the question are the same words found in the text.	**Author and Me:** The answer to the question can be found in the text, but the reader may have to combine two or more parts of the text to arrive at an answer. The words in the question may not directly lead the reader to the answer in the text. The reader has to make connections in order to arrive at an answer.
Think and Search: The answer to the question is not found directly in the text. The reader has to think about the information that the author provided, prior knowledge about the topic, and personal experience. The reader has to make connections in order to answer the question.	**On My Own:** The answer to the question is not found in the text. The reader must use prior knowledge and personal experiences to answer the question. The reader may even be able to answer the question without having read the text, although text information will enhance the response.

Use the following codes to identify the kinds of questions you are being asked:

R = Right There **A = Author and Me**

T = Think and Search **O = On My Own**

Part B Directions: Copy the questions you will be answering in the space below. Then code the question in the column on the right.

Question	Code
1.	
2.	
3.	

Stance Questioning

Directions: Respond to the following questions in order to develop your understanding of the text.

Global Understanding—Being Out and Stepping Into the Text

What is the overall purpose of the text?

What is the most important point in the text?

What details support the most important point?

How do the text features help support the main idea of the text?

Developing an Interpretation—Being In and Moving Through the Text

When were you able to infer the feelings or attitudes of any of the people described in the text?

When were you able to relate concepts or themes to specific information in the text?

Compare two excerpts of significant information from the text.

Identify the cause/effect relationship of important events, concepts, or ideas in the text.

How would the information be different if one of the events or steps described were changed or deleted?

Reflecting on Personal Experiences—Being In and Stepping Out of the Text

What prior knowledge/personal experience can you connect to this topic?

How is the author's point of view on this topic similar to or different from your point of view?

What other information would you like to learn on this topic?

What new information have you gained about this topic and why is this information important to you?

Critical Response—Stepping Out and Analyzing the Reading Experience

How does the author create interest about his or her subject?

Based on the text, what kind of teacher would the author make? Give specific examples. What does the author believe about his or her subject? How do you know?

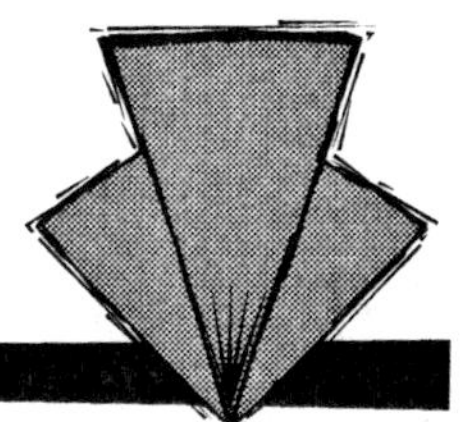

Using a Double-Entry Journal to Wonder

Directions: As you read, record significant information from the text and your questions about what you have read. Use the following sentence starters to get you started with your questions:

I don't understand when. . .
Why did. . .
I'm confused about. . .
How did. . .

Quote, Summary, or Illustration	Questions and Wonderings

Digging Deeper

Directions: Imagine going on an archeological dig to understand text information. Read the text and record key information by copying a significant quote or summarizing important information. Then use the question starters to build your understanding of the concepts or ideas about which you are learning.

Quote or Summary of Text Information	Questions
	I was confused when. . . I want to understand the information about. . . Because. . . I wonder if. . . When I continue reading, I most want to know about. . .

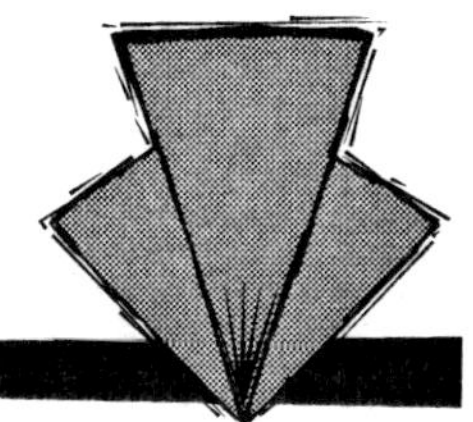

Coding for Quality Questioning

Directions: As you read, use the codes to mark in the margins or on sticky notes next to significant segments of text. Then record your answers to the questions for quality thinking.

T-S = Text-to-Self Questioning

T-T = Text-to-Text Questioning

T-W = Text-to-World Questioning

T-S (Text-to-Self) page____ and paragraph ____ How does the text connect to your personal experiences? How does the text connect to your feelings on the topic?
T-T (Text-to-Text) page _____ and paragraph _____ How does the text connect to other information that you have read in other texts? Does this text information confirm or contradict what you have read in other texts about the same topic? Explain.
T-W (Text-to-World) page _____ and paragraph ______ How does the text connect to what you already know about the topic? How does the text connect to current events?

Concept and Fact T-Chart

Directions: Read the text and record questions that require inferencing, references to concept knowledge, connections to other texts, or further research on the left under the heading for concept questions. Record fact-based questions, right-there questions, and questions about vocabulary on the right, below the heading for fact questions.

Concept Questions	Fact Questions

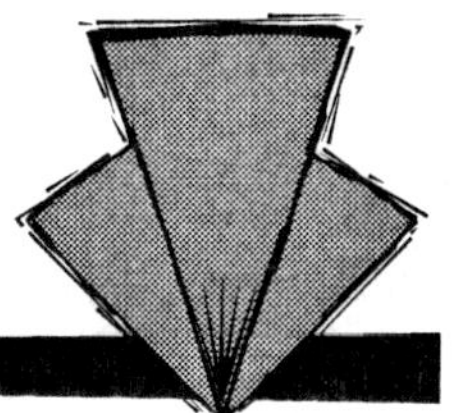

Question Squares

Directions: Read the information and record significant facts from the text. Then write questions for three audiences: teacher, author, and classmates.

Key topic or concept: ______________________________

Facts Related to the Topic	Questions for the Teacher
Questions for the Author	**Questions for the Class**

Questions Before, During, and After

Directions: Record your questions throughout the reading process. Pause at each stage to record speculations and predictions. After you have finished reading, identify more questions and possible answers.

Questions Before Reading	Speculations
Questions During Reading	Predictions
Questions After Reading	Possible Answers

Visualizing

Visualizing

Introduction

Strategic readers visualize during and after reading. These visual images include all the senses, as well as emotions based on the reader's prior knowledge and experience. These visualizations help readers to immerse themselves in the reading, making the details richer and more memorable. Visualizations can be used to draw conclusions, make inferences, and recall important details. Visual images are revised and adapted as the reading continues and new information is uncovered. After sharing visualizations with other readers, the strategic reader will modify and adjust his or her own previous impressions, incorporating the different viewpoints. All of these factors contribute to increased comprehension.

Closely related to inferencing, visualizing requires the reader to make "mind movies," pictures, and sensory impressions based on what has been read. Visualizing strengthens higher-level, divergent thinking. It asks the reader to draw on past experiences and impressions, weaving them into the written text. This technique enables the reader to become more intimately involved with the text and derive meaning. Many studies have demonstrated that when students use visualization strategies, they comprehend better and recall key ideas more effectively. When making abstract concepts more concrete through visualization, students retain the information better.

By teaching students to use visualization and imagery techniques, teachers help students learn more effectively. Students also acquire a strategy to help them assume control of their own learning in the future.

Although visualization is more commonly used in fictional texts, these strategies can be applied to content-area texts as well. Using visualization in science can assist students in learning and retaining complicated concepts, such as cell structure and function, photosynthesis, and mechanical concepts, such as force, speed, and work. In math, visualization can be used to give students a frame of reference when comparing different measurements, such as gram, kilogram, hectogram, and so on. Social studies is an area where visualization can enrich otherwise dry historical facts and motivate students to learn more about a particular period in history.

Visualizing

Inferencing Through Visualization

Visualizing is one of the mental building blocks for proficiency in inferencing. Teachers need to be aware that students can use words from text, titles, charts, diagrams, and illustrations to make inferences and thus improve their ability to understand the information. An effective approach to presenting the idea of inferencing is to share some specific descriptions or scenarios and have students make an inference about the events in the scenario. For example, a seventh grade boy comes home from a baseball game with a smile on his face. His family can infer that he either won the game or made a very good play offensively or defensively. After presenting students with many such scenarios, their confidence with inferencing will improve.

Next, you can move on to inferencing with text. Share with students some descriptive scenarios from the text that create a visual picture in their minds. For example, the author describes a scene where the main character is shopping in the mall. The teacher can lead the students to see many stores, an escalator or elevators, and other shoppers. Filling in the missing information will help students comprehend textual information.

Tapping into Prior Knowledge

Guided practice with previewing text will help students tap into their prior knowledge. Before students begin reading, have them look carefully at the title and identify any visual images associated with its words. Then have them preview the text, noting the headings, subheadings, charts, graphs, and illustrations and identify visual images associated with these various text features. It may help to record these observations on the board. Finally, have students make connections between these visual images and their prior knowledge of the topic. As they read, refer them to their initial visualizations and ask them to revise or clarify their understandings.

Sensory Detail

Proficient readers use sensory details to make pictures in their minds. These readers see, hear, taste, touch, and smell the images that are described in the text. Teachers need to model how to create pictures in one's mind when reading. Proficient readers create mental images but often don't realize what is going on cognitively in order for them to "see" the text. Teachers must help these readers understand the visualizing skills that they have developed in order to build on these skills and, additionally, help struggling readers to use sensory details to begin the process of visualizing text.

Visualizing

Creating Mental Images to Remember Details

Retention is a critical component of reading comprehension. As proficient readers enter the text and begin to form vague pictures of the big ideas, they will also begin to add distinctive impressions of the details. As educators, we often ask students simply to retain the facts, the details, and the small ideas. It is important to teach students that building a strong ability to visualize will help them to retain the big idea(s) and provide the scaffolding on which to hang the details. When we assess students' progress, it is valuable to incorporate many kinds of evaluation. A unit test may include some multiple choice, true/false, short-answer, and long-answer responses. In addition to the traditional approaches to assessment, include a question that asks students to reflect upon how they used visualization to remember key concepts, facts, and details. Such a component of assessment will help them build their metacognitive abilities and ultimately strengthen their retention of information.

Creating Mental Images to Draw Conclusions

Drawing conclusions is a skill essential to all subject areas. When students are able to visualize text information, they are better able to understand the relationship among ideas and draw conclusions about the information that they are learning. One strategy that is very useful in helping students with this skill is to provide them with a "purpose for reading" question that requires them to think about the conclusions that they are drawing as they read. Be sure to have them identify the specific text information that allowed them to draw their conclusions.

Visualizing

Incorporating New Information

One of the key features of learning and teaching is that new information builds on what is already known. If students gain proficiency with linking new information to what they already know about the topic and making connections across contexts and subject areas, then their learning will improve exponentially. The following are some questions that you can ask students to help them build their visualizing skills and to make connections in order to incorporate new information into their existing knowledge base.

Before Reading

What do you already know about the topic?

As you preview the text, what images do you see?

What images do you already have that connect with your current knowledge or understanding of the topic?

Can you describe these images?

Can you represent these images either through art or drama?

During Reading

What new information are you learning about the topic?

What images do you associate with this new information?

Are you visualizing as you read?

Can you describe these images?

How do these new images confirm or contradict the images that you identified before you began reading?

After Reading

What key information (concepts, topics, facts) did you learn?

Have you blended your existing images about the topic with the new images?

Can you represent the connections you have made between your existing knowledge and new knowledge through art, drama, or writing?

How does visualizing improve the learning process?

What strategies did you use to visualize the information you were learning?

How can you apply these strategies in other content areas?

Other questions to help students visualize text are provided on page 263.

Visualizing

Representing Abstract Information as Mental Pictures

One of the most difficult skills is to represent abstract information as a mental picture. For example, if a teacher asks students to read about freedom, he or she may ask them first to identify pictures that come to mind, such as the American flag, the bald eagle, or the Statue of Liberty. As students read, they should be instructed to add to their mental representation by using information from the text.

Using Strategies Independently

What follows is a list of strategies designed to improve students' visualization abilities when reading. Make sure to model how to visualize through think alouds and talk alouds in which you share with students the images you create in your mind as you read and the thinking that accompanies your sense making. Demonstrate for students how to use each strategy on the board and/or overhead. Most importantly, share your enthusiasm for reading and the confusion and misconceptions that you encounter when reading. Gradually release the responsibility for using strategies to students by observing carefully their proficiency and confidence levels with each new strategy you present.

Strategy 1: Double-Entry Journals

Double-entry journals are a very effective tool for building students' metacognitive skills. When working on visualizing, instruct students to read carefully for images, and use the double-entry journal (page 264) to record sensory images on the left side. Then have students draw a picture or describe the images in their heads on the right side. Double-entry journals focusing on abstract concept development (page 265) add an extra dimension to the reading process.

Strategy 2: Text Coding

Having students code text helps them increase their comprehension during reading. Begin by refreshing their memories about the five senses. Share with them the five codes to use for identifying images that appeal to the five senses (an eye for sight, a nose for smell, an ear for sound, a tongue for taste, a hand for touch). Find a short piece of descriptive text, and make an overhead transparency. With an overhead marker, use the appropriate code to mark words, phrases, or sentences that appeal to particular senses. Share the coding worksheet (page 266) with students. Instruct them to read a piece of text, code for sensory detail and then use the worksheet to respond to the sensory images that they identified.

Visualizing

Strategy 3: Listening to Music

Using music is an effective strategy when introducing the skills of visualizing. Classical music, such as the *William Tell Overture* or excerpts from Tchaikovsky's *Nutcracker Suite* will evoke many images in students' minds. Begin by giving them the guide for Listening to Music (page 267) and instructing them to record as many images as possible as they listen to the music. You may need to demonstrate this procedure with a short piece of music. For example, a fast-paced selection of music with a lively rhythm might evoke the image of cowboys riding their horses on the open prairie or fairies dancing in the woods and playing hide-and-seek. After students finish listening to the music and recording their images, have them use the right side of the listening guide to write a brief story, poem, or description that incorporates the images. Emphasize to students that they need to transfer the ability to visualize while listening to music to their reading.

Strategy 4: Text Graphing

Text graphing allows students to visualize the information they are learning as well as evaluate it. This technique is particularly effective to use in social studies classes. Have students list the events that they are encountering in the text. Next, have them think of an artistic representation or symbol for each of the events. Then present them with the activity on page 268 and have them evaluate each of the events by drawing their symbols to correspond with the appropriate number on the graph. For example, the American's defeat of the British at the Battle of Yorktown might be evaluated as a +4 because of the American's victory but not receive a +5 rating because many lives were lost in the process. It is important to note that there are not any right or wrong answers in text graphing and that different students may rate events differently. Students should be encouraged to justify their ratings either in writing or small-group or whole-group discussions.

Visualizing

Strategy 5: Parts-of-Speech Visualizing

This simple technique reinforces parts of speech and requires students to categorize the images they are encountering. Present them with the parts-of-speech organizer (page 269) and have them record specific nouns, vivid verbs, interesting adjectives and adverbs, and prepositional phrases as they read. After completing that section of the worksheet, students evaluate the author's word choice.

Strategy 6: Predicting and Inferencing Charts

Predicting, inferencing, and visualizing are skills that overlap in the repertoire of essential proficiencies that good readers must have. Use the Predicting and Inferencing Chart (page 270) to have students read and record images in the left column. After they record these images, have them make predictions about what will happen next. Finally, instruct them to draw inferences based on the images and predictions they have made. Guide them toward inferences that connect to the larger concepts they are studying. This technique works particularly well with social studies and science concepts and topics.

Strategy 7: Rotating Dramas

Pair students with a partner and instruct each to take on the role of a different character from the text. Then have them interact with each other through dialogue or movement. This interaction should take no longer than a minute or two and will create a vivid image in students' minds regarding the relationships between the people, ideas, or concepts in their reading. This technique works across all content areas. For example, the characters in social studies may be historical figures or people who live in other countries; the characters in science may be chemicals, elements, or scientific concepts; the characters in math may be numbers, signs, or symbols. The pairs should present their dramas to the class.

Strategy 8: Tableaux Dramas

A tableaux is a frozen scene from the text and is a non-threatening way to get every student in the class interacting with text. Students need to work with a partner or in groups to create a tableaux. Assign each group a different portion of text to dramatize. Students work cooperatively to create a frozen scene that depicts the relationship between people, ideas, or concepts from the text. There is no dialogue in a tableaux, although students may choose to have their characters engage in a repetitive movement to show some particular feature of the idea or concept they are dramatizing. After students have created their tableaux, they should perform them in front of the class. A variation of this strategy has the class guessing which part of the text they are dramatizing.

Visualizing

Strategy 9: Mini-Dramas

Mini-dramas allow students in teams or pairs to summarize what they have learned in an interactive way. Have them use the planning sheets (pages 271 and 272) to identify characters, concepts, and facts that they will incorporate into their mini-dramas. Then instruct them to plan a brief dialogue that demonstrates the relationship(s) between ideas. Mini-dramas are a great technique to help students build their visualization skills. The teams or pairs present their dramas to the class.

Strategy 10: Talk Shows

Planning a talk show will get students involved in writing dialogues, developing opinions, and interviewing characters in order to demonstrate their knowledge of a particular concept or idea. Have them use the worksheet (page 273) to plan their talk show in cooperative groups. These groups will then present their talk shows to the class.

Strategy 11: Symbolic Story Representations

Symbolic story representations (P. Enciso, 1992) involve a technique in which students are given different pieces of colored construction paper and use the paper to tear shapes that represent different ideas, concepts, or characters from the text. Then they arrange the shapes on a large piece of construction paper in order to show the relationships between or among the ideas. Finally, students explain their creations in small groups or through a written response. The simple act of tearing shapes is highly motivating and is a non-threatening way for them to represent their ideas since little to no artistic ability is required.

Strategy 12: Storyboarding

An essential step in the planning process of movies and TV shows, storyboarding is a great way for students to visualize the sequence of steps in a scientific experiment or the events that unfolded during a particular time in history. Introduce the idea of storyboarding to students by showing them the Storyboard Planner worksheet (page 274) and having them think about a sequence of events or steps with which they are familiar. For example, they can think of their morning routine before coming to school. Then have students read the text and illustrate through symbols and simple illustrations the sequence or steps in the text. Students may work in small groups or pairs and present their storyboards to the class.

Visualizing

Strategy 13: Differentiated Instruction

Middle school students thrive on differentiated instruction. Create different corners of the classroom that are dedicated to different learning styles. One corner of the classroom could be called the "Dramatic Dugout." In this corner, provide space for three to four performers and three to four audience members. The Dramatic Dugout should have multiple texts, dramatic scenarios, and supplies for making scenery and props. Another corner could be called "Discussion Detour." In this corner, provide for four to six students to engage in a discussion about the texts they are reading. This corner should have multiple texts, discussion frames, and sentence starters, as well as a tape recorder so that students can tape their discussions and reflect on their communication skills. A third corner could be titled the "Artist's Arena" and provide a rich supply of art materials so that students can create representations of the texts they are reading. The final corner could be titled "Writer's Retreat" and include space and supplies for four to eight writers to reflect on their reading or create their own text representing key ideas and concepts they are learning.

Strategy 14: Making Postcards

Having students visualize various audiences helps them to strengthen their reading skills. Instruct them to use pages 275 and 276 to create a postcard that demonstrates a relationship between characters or ideas in the text. Students will have to use their inferencing skills to conceive of such an interaction and use their visualization skills to imagine the sender, receiver, and location that the postcard depicts. In social studies, examples include the creation of postcards between historical figures. In science, examples include postcards that show the interaction between neutrons and protons, veins and arteries, or animals that occupy the same habitat. This activity can also be done by providing students with 4" x 6" (10 cm x 15 cm) blank index cards. On one side students write the message and address, and on the other side they can draw a picture representing the subject, event, or place.

Strategy 15: Using Poetry to Create Movies in the Mind

Poetry is an excellent method for activating visualization. A guided visualization session with students might go something like this:

Teacher: Before we get started, I want you to get into a comfortable position at your desks. I want you to sit straight but relaxed with your hands folded in front of you on your desk. Take a deep breath through your nose, and then slowly let it out through your mouth. Let's do that a few times. Slowly inhale through the nose; exhale through the mouth. I'm going to read something to you now, and I want you to listen carefully. As you are listening with your eyes closed, I want you to picture in your mind what is happening. Be sure to think not only about how things look, but also how they sound, feel, smell. Think about the emotions you are feeling as you visualize the events as they unfold.

The teacher then reads the poem "The Zephyr Queen" by Ilyse McKennaugh (page 277) without commentary or interpretation.

Teacher: I'm going to re-read parts of this poem, and I want you to imagine that you are watching a movie about what is happening. Close your eyes and picture in your mind a movie that shows what is going on.

Visualizing

Strategy 15: Using Poetry to Create Moves in the Mind (cont.)

Teacher reads:

It was one of those rare summer days,

When it wasn't too hot,

Nor too steamy.

The air was pure and fresh,

As I lay on the dewy grass,

Green and sweet-smelling.

And I watched.

The sky above went up into forever,

While breezes brushed my hair,

And the sun's rays caressed my face,

And the world was clean and new.

Teacher: Who would like to describe the movie that you see?

Student #1: I think about when my Dad and I are going hunting.

Student #2: I see our vacation last year when we went to Yosemite Park. It was so green there!

Teacher: Those are some good mind movies! Does anyone see himself or herself in the movie?

Student #3: Yeah! I see myself walking down a dirt road behind my grandma's house. She lives out in the country.

Teacher: You bring up a good point. Everyone who has shared his or her mind movies has described something that is out in the country, out in nature. What words made you think it was out in the country?

Student #4: When you said the sky was high and the grass was green and everything was so clean. That made me think of being out in the woods.

Teacher: Good observation. Now I want all of you to close your eyes again and in your minds, go back to that movie you started. Listen to the next part:

Cotton candy clouds were fantasy creatures
From a long-ago time when knights battled dragons
For the hands of their Ladies.
A floating scrap of black velvet caught my eye.

Strategy 15: Using Poetry to Create Moves in the Mind *(cont.)*

High above the earth,
Floating downward,
Ever closer.
I recognized her regal form.
Her wings conveying her without effort,
Like Cleopatra on the royal barge,
Floating on a Nile of clouds.

Teacher: Has anyone added something to his or her mind movies?

Student #5: Yeah! When you said there was something black floating in the sky, I started thinking about a big, black bird. Maybe a crow or something.

Student #6: Me too! I saw a bird in my movie, but to me it was a hawk.

Student #7: You guys are both wrong! It was an eagle; they have white heads.

Student #6: How do you know it had a white head? I don't remember hearing that! Are you sure?

Teacher: You all have good ideas—let's read on to find out what kind of bird it really is. I'm gong to read some more, and I again want you to close your eyes, and add to the movie you have started in your mind. Remember, if you need to change some of the details about your movie, it's perfectly fine to do that.

Teacher reads:

She wheeled ever nearer,
Her keen gaze never faltering from her prey,
When a cloud monster surrounded her,
Snatched her up in its claws.
And the sun's rays caressed my face,
And the world was clean and new.

Teacher: What have you added to your mind movie?

Student #5: I've changed my mind—it isn't a crow. I think it IS an eagle!

Teacher: What made you change your mind?

Student #5: When you said the part about the bird having white on his head. Crows are all black, but eagles have white on their heads.

Visualizing

Strategy 15: Using Poetry to Create Moves in the Mind (cont.)

Teacher: Great attention to details. It is OK to change your opinion when you have more facts. Anything else?

Student #7: Well, I pictured the bird getting lost in the clouds. Then I couldn't see it anymore.

Teacher: What was it that made you think it was lost in the clouds?

Student #7: The part about the cloud that was shaped like a monster grabbed the bird. I know it didn't really eat the bird; it was just my imagination because the cloud looked like a monster.

Teacher: Excellent interpretation of a metaphor! When the author says, "a cloud monster," she doesn't mean a real dragon, does she? I'm glad you picked up on that. Now let's add some more to our mind movies:

> *Shielding my eyes,*
>
> *I watched,*
>
> *I waited,*
>
> *Then I saw her.*
>
> *Again a scrap of black velvet*
>
> *As she escaped the cloud monster.*
>
> *Becoming ever smaller,*
>
> *Farther away.*
>
> *Then she was gone.*

Student #8: I see the eagle coming out of the clouds, but now it's farther away!

Teacher: Let's listen to the last part and add it to your mind movie:

> *And on days when the snow drifts high*
>
> *Outside my window,*
>
> *I sit by the fire,*
>
> *Recalling the Zephyr Queen.*
>
> *And I remember that*
>
> *The sun's rays caressed my face,*
>
> *And the world was clean and new.*

Strategy 15: Using Poetry to Create Moves in the Mind (cont.)

Student #8: Yeah, it's an eagle. The rest of you weren't listening.
Teacher: You have a good memory, but it's all right when people need to read or hear something again so that they can visualize what's going on. If I told you the word "zephyr" means a soft and gentle wind, what does that tell you about the subject of the poem?

Student #5: It makes me imagine an eagle even more because they fly and glide so smoothly. So an eagle would be a king or a queen of the winds and the air.

Teacher: Good interpretation. Now, would anyone like to share with us his or her entire movie?

Student #3: Well, I'm walking along the dirt road behind my grandma's house. She lives on a farm and there are a lot of wild animals around. Sometimes we see deer and raccoons and stuff. I'm walking along and I look up into the sky and I see this huge eagle! I'm excited about it because I've never seen a wild eagle before. I stop and watch it fly; it's so bright that I have to shade my eyes from the sun. The eagle flies and soars in the sky—it looks like my remote control plane—and then it flies into some clouds; and I don't see it anymore. I keep watching, though, and before long, it comes out of the clouds. Now it's farther away, and I guess it's flying back to its nest somewhere. Maybe it's hunting for food for baby eagles. Hey—does the father eagle take care of the babies, or just the mother? Anyway, I watch it until I can't see it anymore; then I run back to my grandma's. I can't wait to tell her and grandpa about it.

Teacher: That's a very RICH mind movie! So many details. Thanks for sharing that with us. It was interesting to me that you mentioned that you had never seen a wild eagle before. I never have either. The only place I have ever seen a live eagle is at the zoo. I read somewhere that very few people ever get to see wild eagles. Does anyone know why?

At this point, the teacher can launch into a science lesson about endangered species, the use of pesticides, wildlife conservation, etc. This is a great way not only to help students visualize concepts that they are learning, but also to activate prior knowledge and set a purpose for learning. An activity like this one helps to engage students' imagination and gets them talking about their thoughts.

When choosing poems that deal with content-area subjects, look for those that have simple language and evoke strong images.

Visualizing

Strategy 15: Using Poetry to Create Moves in the Mind (cont.)

Other content-area poems suitable for visualization practice include:

"Paul Revere's Ride" by Henry Wadsworth Longfellow (social studies)

"Oh Captain! My Captain!" by Walt Whitman (social studies)

"I, Too" by Langston Hughes (social studies)

"Concord Hymn" by Ralph Waldo Emerson (social studies)

"The New Colossus" by Emma Lazarus (social studies)

"A Country Boy in Winter" by Sarah Orne Jewett (science & nature)

"Dawn" by William Carlos Williams (science & nature)

"The Great Figure" by William Carlos Williams (fire safety)

"The Tulip Bed" by William Carlos Williams (science & nature)

"The Snowing of the Pines" by Thomas Wentworth Higginson (science & nature)

"The West Wind" by John Masefield (science & nature)

"Bagley Wood" by Lionel Johnson (science & nature)

"A Child's Garden of Verses" by Robert Louis Stevenson (science & nature)

"Helen Keller" by Edmund Clarence Stedman (social studies)

"Landing of the Pilgrims" by Felicia Dorothea Hermans (social studies)

"The Cloud" by Percy Bysshe Shelley (science & nature)

"Afternoon on a Hill" by Edna St. Vincent Millay (science & nature)

"Heat" by Hilda Doolittle (science & nature)

"The Rain" by W.H. Davies (science & nature)

"Never and Forever" by George Charles Selden (science & nature)

"The Twelve Months" by George Ellis (seasons)

"October" by Paul Laurence Dunbar (seasons)

"Fog" by Carl Sandburg (weather)

Whenever using poetry for visualization and activation of prior knowledge, always remember to bring the lesson back to the moment and relate what has been discussed to the topic at hand. This strategy will facilitate the bridging of knowledge from one area to another.

Questions for Visualizing Text

Directions: Use the following questions to help you visualize the text.
What pictures are you forming in your mind of people, places, things, and ideas?

What details from the text are helping you to create a picture in your mind?

What details from your own experience are you adding to the picture in your own mind?

If you were to make a movie using the pictures in your mind, what would you use for background music?

If you were to make a movie using the pictures in your mind, what colors and shading would you use to represent mood?

Are you seeing in your mind what the author intended you to see? Why do you think so?

How would you describe the pictures or images in your mind to a friend?

Do you see yourself interacting with the people, places, things, or ideas that you are visualizing in your mind? Explain.

What images or details are missing from the text? Can you fill in these images in your own mind?

Do the images, based on text information, that you see in your mind remind you of a personal memory? Explain.

Do the images and ideas in your mind remind you of other texts that you have read on the same topic? Explain.

What if a major idea in the text were deleted? How would this deletion change the pictures in your mind?

If you were to paint a picture of a major idea from the text, what would it look like? What colors and textures would you use?

Imagine a dialogue between people or ideas in the text. What are the contents of the dialogue and the voice tones of the people/ideas?

How does visualizing ideas from the text help you to make inferences?

Visualization Double-Entry Journal

Directions: As you read, record a passage that includes many sensory details and then either draw or describe the image that is in your head. In the first column, quote or list sensory details from the text. Then provide a drawing that shows what is in your head or a description that includes details that are not in the text.

Details	Illustrations

Visualizing Abstract Information

Directions: As you read, record information about the concept or topic that you are studying. Use a quote or words that represent the concept or idea in the text. Then draw a picture of what you see in your mind as you read.

Quote or Words	Illustration

My response: This image reminds me of. . .

Text Coding and Visualizing

Directions: As you read, use the following codes to mark in the margins or on a sticky note next to significant segments of text. Then use the following chart to record your answers to the questions for quality visualizing.

- Picture of an eye—details that appeal to sight
- Picture of a nose—details that appeal to smell
- Picture of an ear—details that appeal to sound
- Picture of a tongue—details that appeal to taste
- Picture of a hand—details that appeal to touch

Details from the Text (Use the text coding to find text information.)	**Response** (Choose from the sentence starters below to get you started on your response.) • This image reminds me of. . . • The details from my own mind that I added to the text information include. . . • The author included these details in order to. . . • I wonder. . .

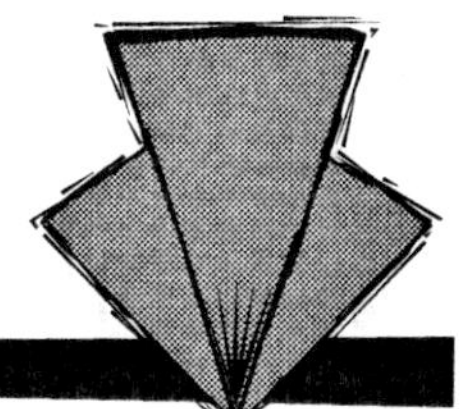

Listening to Music

Directions: As you listen to the music, record as many images as you can in the left side of the chart. When the music is finished, use the right side to write a response using the images. This response can be in the form of a creative short story, a poem, or a description of a memory. Be creative and descriptive.

Images from the Music	**Response** (short story, poem, description of a memory, etc.)

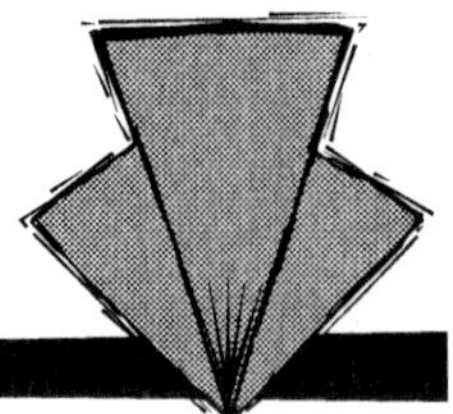

Text Graphing

Directions: Illustrate the events in the text. Events that are positive are to be illustrated in the top half of the chart and events that are negative are to be illustrated in the bottom half of the chart. Use the +5 to -5 rating system to indicate the degree of positive or negative associated with the event. The center horizontal line is "0."

+5
+4
+3
+2
+1
-1
-2
-3
-4
-5

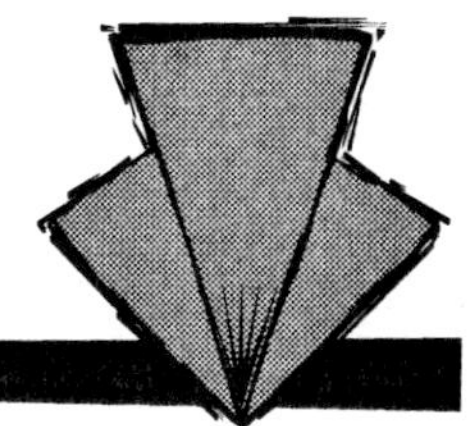

Parts-of-Speech Visualizing

Directions: As you are reading, record specific nouns, vivid verbs, interesting adjectives or adverbs, and helpful prepositional phrases.

Specific Nouns	Vivid Verbs
Interesting Adjectives and Adverbs	**Prepositional Phrases**

Do you think the author did a good job of creating a picture in your head using different parts of speech? Explain.

____

____

____

____

____

Predicting and Inferencing Chart

Directions: Record key images from the text. Then make predictions and inferences by using the guiding questions provided for you.

Images from the Text	**Predicting:** What will the author include next about the topic?

Inferencing: How does the text information connect to the major concept you are studying?

____

____

____

____

____

____

____

____

Drama Planner

Directions: With your team member(s), plan out a mini-drama that shows what you have learned.

Student Names	Characters	Main Character Traits

Key concept(s) you will dramatize: ____

____

____

Facts from your learning: ____

____

____

____

____

____

____

____

____

____

____

____

Drama Planner *(cont.)*

Dialogue that shows key concepts, facts learned, and relationships among ideas. (Use the back of this page if you need more space.)

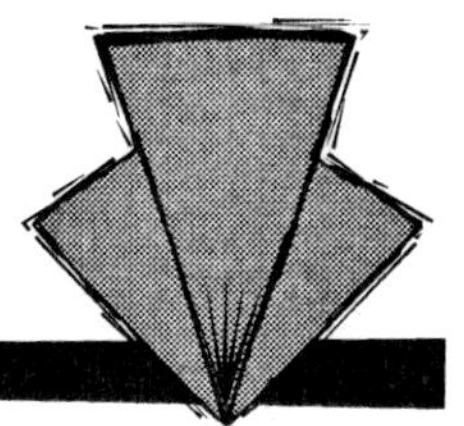

Talk Show Planner

Directions: With your team plan a talk show that shows the knowledge you have gained about the topic or concept you are studying.

Student Names	Talk Show Host(s)	Talk Show Guest(s)

Visual aids that will be used in the talk show to illustrate the topics learned:

____

____

____

Each of the talk show participants will have to plan a talk show that illustrates information about the topic(s) in the text. Each member will want to use separate lined notebook paper to plan and write the talk show. Use the following questions to guide you:

1. Who are the main characters in the talk show? (historical figures in social studies; chemicals or elements in science; signs or symbols in mathematics)
2. What is their interaction? What is the problem?
3. When did this interaction or problem occur?
4. Where did the important information take place?
5. Why is the information important?
6. What is the overall message that the talk show host wants the audience to gain?

Storyboard Planner

Directions: Illustrate the events, process, or steps as they occurred in the text.

Event #1	Event #2	Event #3
Event #4	**Event #5**	**Event #6**
Event #7	**Event #8**	**Event #9**
Event #10	**Event #11**	**Event #12**

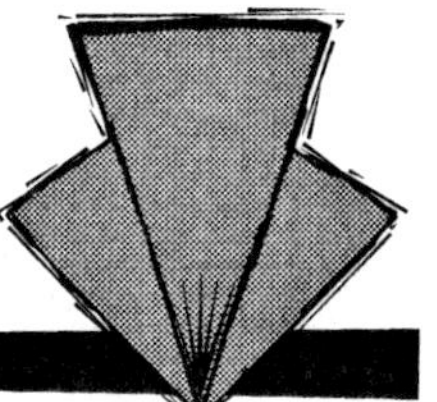

Making a Postcard

Directions: Plan a postcard that is sent from one person or idea in the text to another person or idea. Use the front of the card (below) to draw the location from which the postcard is sent. Use the back of the card (page 399) to describe the location, write the message, draw an appropriate stamp and cancellation stamp, and write the address to which it is being sent.

Front of Postcard

Making a Postcard *(cont.)*

Back of Postcard

Description of setting

(Message)

(Stamp)

(Address)

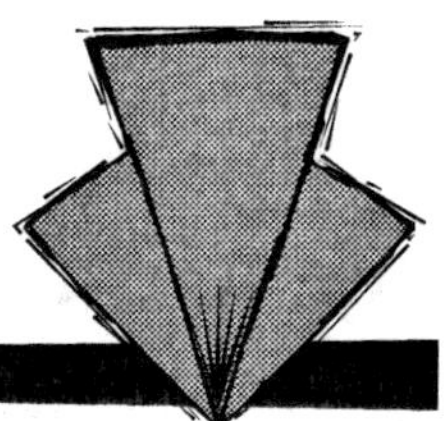

Zephyr Queen

by Ilyse McKennaugh

It was one of those rare summer days,
When it wasn't too hot,
Nor too steamy.
The air was pure and fresh,
As I lay on the dewy grass,
Green and sweet-smelling.
And I watched.
The sky above went up into forever,
While breezes brushed my hair,
And the sun's rays caressed my face,
And the world was clean and new.

Cotton candy clouds were fantasy creatures
From a long-ago time when knights battled dragons
For the hands of their Ladies.
A floating scrap of black velvet caught my eye.
High above the earth,
Floating downward,
Ever closer.
I recognized her regal form.
Her wings conveying her without effort,
Like Cleopatra on the royal barge,
Floating on a Nile of clouds.
And the sun's rays caressed my face,
And the world was clean and new.

As I watched her solitary passage,
The sun flashed
On her Crown of white feathers.
She wheeled ever nearer,
Her keen gaze never faltering from her prey,
When a cloud monster surrounded her,
Snatched her up in its claws.
And the sun's rays caressed my face,
And the world was clean and new.

Shielding my eyes,
I watched,
I waited,
Then I saw her.
Again a scrap of black velvet
As she escaped the cloud monster.
Becoming ever smaller,
Farther away.
Then she was gone.
And on days when the snow drifts high
Outside my window,
I sit by the fire,
Recalling the Zephyr Queen.
And I remember that
The sun's rays caressed my face,
And the world was clean and new.

CD Index

Graphic Organizers in *Microsoft Word*

Page Number	Title	Filename
20	Box Web	23.dot
21	Connecting the Main Idea and Supporting Details to Prior Knowledge	25.dot
22	Responding to Supporting Details	27.dot
23	Novelty Notetaking	29.dot
24	Retelling and Reacting	31.dot
41	Using the 5Ws + H	53.dot
42	Key Word Notetaking	55.dot
60	Roots/Prefixes/Suffixes	79.dot
62	Charting Characteristics	83.dot
63	Personal Association Vocabulary Strategy	85.dot
64	Vocabulary Explorations Through Questioning	87.dot
65	Text Coding and Vocabulary	89.dot
67	Personification Vocabulary	93.dot
68	Exploring Content Vocabulary	95.dot
69	Dictionary Definitions	97.dot
81	Previewing and Self-Questioning	109.dot
82	K-W-L and K-W-L Plus	111.dot
83	Agree or Disagree Anticipation Guide	113.dot
84	True or False Anticipation Guide	115.dot
86	Riveting Reflections	119.dot
87	Predicting and Confirming Guide	121.dot
88	Visual Reading Guide	123.dot
90	Synthesizing Opinions	127.dot
91	Extending What You Have Learned	129.dot
92	Partnered Reading	131.dot
104	Fact/Opinion Partner Chart	143.dot
113	Evaluating Author's Voice	161.dot
123	Description Tree	171.dot
124	Compare/Contrast Organizer I	173.dot
125	Compare/Contrast Organizer II	175.dot
127	Comparison Matrix	179.dot
128	Cause and Effect Organizer	181.dot
129	If/Then Organizer	183.dot
130	Sequence Chain	185.dot
131	Problem/Solution Organizer	187.dot
132	Proposition/Support Organizer	189.dot
133	Time Line	191.dot
146	Using the Chapter Title for Before, During, and After Reading	205.dot
148	Prediction Chart	209.dot
149	Bold and Italicized Words	211.dot
150	Identifying Topic Sentences	213.dot
151	Summary Sentences	215.dot
152	Evaluating Text Organizers	217.dot
153	Evaluating Graphic Features	219.dot
154	Evaluating Author's Purpose	221.dot
155	Choosing the Right Text Organizer	223.dot
156	Comparing Two Texts	225.dot
157	Add a Text Organizer	227.dot

CD Index

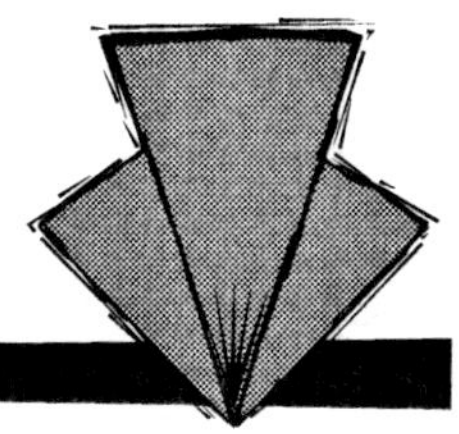

Graphic Organizers in *Microsoft Word* (cont.)

Page Number	Title	Filename
158	Partnered Reading	229.dot
170	Using the Foreword	241.dot
171	Table of Contents Questions	243.dot
172	Using a Glossary	245.dot
173	Creating an Illustrated Mini-Glossary	247.dot
174	The Appendix	249.dot
175	Investigating the Index	251.dot
176	Team Book Investigation	253.dot
177	Evaluating the Parts of a Nonfiction Book	255.dot
178	Text Coding	257.dot
179	Analyzing the Author's Choices	259.dot
180	Locating Information with a Partner	261.dot
191	Conveying Underlying Meanings	271.dot
192	Inferencing About the Author	273.dot
194	Identifying the "Text in My Head"	277.dot
195	Text Coding for Inferential Thinking	279.dot
196	Conceptual Inferencing	281.dot
197	Global Inferencing	283.dot
198	Insightful Interpretations	285.dot
199	Partnered Reading	287.dot
200	Perceptive Predictions	289.dot
201	Text Feature Inferencing	291.dot
212	Evaluating Purpose	303.dot
213	Text Coding for Purpose	305.dot
214	Question/Answer	307.dot
215	Question/Answer/Opinion	309.dot
217	Author and Me Analysis	313.dot
218	Purpose and Analyzing the Author	315.dot
219	Purpose and Solving Problems	317.dot
220	Reading and Skimming for Facts	319.dot
221	Purpose and Being Persuaded	321.dot
222	Purpose and Extending Prior Knowledge	323.dot
223	Purpose and Following Directions	325.dot
224	Partnered Reading	327.dot
241	Using a Double-Entry Journal to Wonder	347.dot
242	Digging Deeper	349.dot
243	Coding for Quality Questioning	351.dot
244	Concept and Fact T-Chart	353.dot
245	Question Squares	355.dot
246	Questions Before, During, After	357.dot
264	Visualization Double-Entry Journal	375.dot
265	Visualizing Abstract Information	377.dot
266	Text Coding and Visualizing	379.dot
267	Listening to Music	381.dot
268	Text Graphing	383.dot
269	Parts-of-Speech Visualizing	385.dot
270	Predicting and Inferencing Chart	387.dot

CD Index

Graphic Organizers in *Microsoft Word* *(cont.)*

Page Number	Title	Filename
271	Drama Planner	389.dot
273	Talk Show Planner	393.dot
274	Storyboard Planner	395.dot
275	Making a Postcard (Front)	397.dot
276	Making a Postcard (Back)	399.dot

Graphic Organizers in *Inspiration*

Page Number	Title	Filename
123	Description Tree	171.ins
125	Compare/Contrast Organizer II	175.ins
128	Cause and Effect Organizer	181.ins
129	If/Then Organizer	183.ins
130	Sequence Chain	185.ins

Notes:

Notes: